THE REMINISCENCES OF
Captain Wilma Leona Jackson
Nurse Corps, U.S. Navy (Retired)

INTERVIEWED BY
Paul Stillwell

U.S. Naval Institute • Annapolis, Maryland

Copyright © 1999

Preface

In the autumn of 1986, a group of former Navy nurses held a reunion in the Washington, D.C., area. Ms. Martha Crawley, who was then on the staff of the Naval Historical Center in Washington, had earlier indicated to me that a particularly impressive member of the nurses' group was Captain Leona Jackson, who had been a prisoner of the Japanese during World War II. Martha had heard some of Captain Jackson's recollections during a previous meeting and suggested that I record them on tape for the benefit of history. In 1986 I did just that, sitting down with Captain Jackson during the course of her visit to the East.

The interview was an excellent one, providing examples of Captain Jackson's extremely high standards, her leadership qualities, conscientious approach to her duties, and an intellectual curiosity that stimulated her to learn about many other subjects besides those involved with her chosen profession. When we met, she expressed the hope that I could come visit her home, Lilac Hill, in Union, Ohio. We would then be able to record the memories of the remainder of her career, capping the followup interviews with a discussion of her service as Director of the Navy Nurse Corps.

When I contacted Captain Jackson subsequently, she asked for a delay so she could do a better job of getting her place into shape. She wanted it to reflect the sense of order and discipline that was her hallmark. We finally arranged an appointment for February of 1989. When I arrived at her house in Ohio, it was apparent that the aging process had taken a toll on her. Her mind no longer had the high degree of sharpness I had observed two and a half years earlier. We attempted another interview to carry the story of her career forward, but she wasn't up to it. However, thanks to the courtesy of Captain Jackson's son William, we are able to make available the transcript of that first interview, and it is a gem, describing the early years of her career as a nurse. Especially interesting is the account of her service on Guam, capture by the Japanese, and return to the United States. Throughout the interview, she demonstrated herself to be a caring person, one who had gone out of her way to meet the needs of her patients.

Mr. Jan Herman, historian for the Navy's Bureau of Medicine and Surgery, has been most helpful throughout the process of preparing this transcript for release. He provided useful information for incorporation in the finished product; included, for example, is a copy of an interview then-Lieutenant (junior grade) Jackson did following her return from Japan to the United States. I have done some slight editing of the transcript in the interests of smoothness and clarity, but it is quite close to the original spoken version. I have also inserted some footnotes to provide additional information. Ms. Ann Hassinger of the Institute's history division has made a significant contribution to the project through her diligence in the overall process of printing, proofreading, and overseeing the binding of the completed volume.

Paul Stillwell
Director, History Division
U.S. Naval Institute
June 1999

CAPTAIN WILMA LEONA JACKSON
NURSE CORPS, UNITED STATES NAVY (RETIRED)

Wilma Leona Jackson was born in Union, Ohio, on 1 September 1909, the daughter of Roy A. and Carrie J. Class. She attended elementary schools there and was graduated from Butler Centralized School in Vandalia, Ohio, in 1927. She then entered the Nurses Training School of Miami Valley Hospital, Dayton, Ohio, and was graduated on 9 September 1930. She attended George Washington University, Washington, D.C., and Columbia University, New York, New York. She holds bachelor of science and master of arts degrees from the latter.

Appointed to the Nurse Corps of the U.S. Navy on 6 July 1936, she was subsequently promoted to lieutenant (junior grade) in February 1943; lieutenant, November 1944; lieutenant commander, April 1946; commander, October 1953, to date from 1 September 1952; and captain, 1 May 1954, when she assumed the duties of Director of the Navy Nurse Corps.

Reporting for active duty in July 1936, she served first at the Naval Hospital, Philadelphia, Pennsylvania, and then on 5 July 1939 was transferred to the Naval Hospital, Brooklyn, New York. In October 1940 she was ordered to Mare Island, California, and after a brief duty at the naval hospital there, reported to the U.S. Naval Hospital, Guam, Marianas Islands. When Guam fell to the Japanese in December 1941, she was taken prisoner of war. Transferred as a prisoner of war to Japan in January 1942, she was returned to the United States on the Swedish liner Gripsholm, via Lourenço Marques, Portuguese East Africa, arriving in the United States in August 1942 with the first exchange of the diplomatic staffs and other nationals of Japan and the United States.

Reporting to the Office of Naval Officer Procurement, Navy Department, Washington, D.C., she first had duty in connection with nurse procurement during the period October 1942 to April 1944, and for eight months thereafter in the Bureau of Medicine and Surgery, Nurse Corps Personnel Division. In December 1944 she reported to Fleet Hospital #103, Guam Island, and from January to December 1945 served as senior Nurse Corps officer in the island command. She received a letter of commendation, with authorization to wear the commendation ribbon, from the Commander in Chief Pacific Fleet, as follows:

"For meritorious service while serving as Supervisor, U.S. Navy Nurse, Guam, Marianas Islands, from 19 January to 2 September 1945. Lieutenant Jackson was of outstanding assistance in solving many trying problems in a period of unsettled conditions during early hospital construction and development on Guam. She rendered valuable service in the supervision of assignment of nurses to U.S. Navy and Military Government hospitals, the efficient coordination of Nurse Corps activities in those hospitals and the liaison established between the Island Medical Office and the four U.S. Army hospitals on Guam. Her initiative, sound judgment and professional knowledge were important factors during the Iwo Jima and Okinawa Campaigns when large numbers of casualties were received on Guam, severely taxing the available hospital facilities. Her conduct and devotion to duty were an inspiration to all with whom she served and at all times in keeping with the highest traditions of the U.S. Naval Service."

Upon her return to the United States, she again served in the Navy Department, 16 months in the Naval Dispensary, and from June 1947 until June 1950 as Education Officer in the Bureau of Medicine and Surgery. She attended Columbia University, New York City, from July 1950 until June 1952, when she was assigned to the U.S. Naval Hospital, Oakland, California, where she served as Assistant Chief Nurse until 5 December 1953. On 29 December she reported to the Naval Hospital, Portsmouth, Virginia, for duty as Chief Nurse. She assumed the duty of Director of the Navy Nurse Corps on 1 May 1954 and remained in the capacity until 1958. She retired from active duty in May 1958.

Captain Jackson's decorations included the following: Commendation Ribbon, the American Defense Service Medal, Asiatic-Pacific Campaign Medal, American Campaign Medal, World War II Victory Medal, and the National Defense Service Medal.

Captain Jackson died at the age of 88 on 23 March 1998 at the VA Hospice in Dayton, Ohio.

Authorization

The U.S. Naval Institute is hereby authorized to make available to individuals, libraries, and other repositories of its choosing the transcripts of an oral history interview concerning the life and career of Captain Leona M. Jackson, Nurse Corps, U.S. Navy (Retired) The interview was recorded on 26 September 1986 in collaboration with Paul Stillwell for the U.S. Naval Institute.

The undersigned does hereby release and assign to the U.S. Naval Institute the rights and title to these interviews, with the exception that the relatives of the interviewee retain the right to use the material for their own purposes, as they see fit. The copyright in both the oral and transcribed versions shall be the property of the U.S. Naval Institute. The tape recordings of the interviews are and will remain the property of the U.S. Naval Institute.

Signed and sealed this 5th day of August 1996.

William R. Jackson - Guardian of Capt. Leona Jackson
William Jackson, on behalf of Leona M. Jackson
Captain, Nurse Corps, U.S. Navy (Retired)

Interview with Captain W. Leona Jackson, Nurse Corps, U.S. Navy (Retired)

Place: Twin Bridges Marriott, Arlington, Virginia

Date: Friday, 26 September 1986

Interviewer: Paul Stillwell

Paul Stillwell: Captain, to begin at the beginning. I know you have a great interest in the background and history of your family, so perhaps you could provide some of that before we get into your own life and career.

Captain Jackson: Yes. Well, we can. But I thought it would be more interesting and probably would raise some more questions as you saw it. And that was why I wanted to give you the opportunity, if you wished, to come to Lilac Hill when I get it put back together again.*

Paul Stillwell: All right.

Captain Jackson: Then I'll take you around and show you my home territory.

Paul Stillwell: All right, good.

Captain Jackson: I've seen a lot of the world, but you'll notice I went back home.

Paul Stillwell: Well, perhaps you could begin then with some of your own earliest memories.

---

* Lilac Hill was the name for Captain Jackson's home in Union, Ohio. Unfortunately, by the time an interview was held there in early 1989, her health had declined to such a degree that the interview was not a productive one for the sake of history.

Captain Jackson: Well, to go back to this matter, the fact that Butler Township High School had four years in Latin, where the Randolph Township High School was in the area in which we lived, just about five miles from Vandalia, where my grandparents lived, had only two years. I figured that for any one of those three professions, four years of Latin would be a good background, because a great deal of your medical terminology is Latin, and a lot of your legal terminology is Latin.

Now, granted that in 1927, when I graduated from high school, there weren't many women lawyers, but Ohio had Judge Florence Allen. She was the only woman judge, I think, in the federal system at that point.

Paul Stillwell: And you were keeping your options open then.

Captain Jackson: I was keeping my options open, and then later on in high school I decided that it was going to be nursing. I enjoyed people. I've always enjoyed working with them, and it appealed to me. And I have never regretted that. I've added to it a great deal, as the years have gone by, because there are so many other areas that move into it in dealing with people.

Paul Stillwell: Were there any specific individuals who served as a stimulus or inspiration to go into nursing?

Captain Jackson: No. There were a number of graduates. In fact, one of my classmates and I were roommates at Miami Valley Hospital School of Nursing for a while. Then she did not pass her probationary period. She didn't have quite the emotional stability that--our director at that particular time was a graduate of Vassar and of the Army School of Nursing. During World War I the Army had a school of nursing. And, of course, she was pretty strict in her selection, and Dorothy had had a medium record in high school. I had been one of two competing people for the top grade in high school. It was not a large class; it was a class of 28. And this had to do with the admission to the school of nursing, don't you see.

Paul Stillwell: Yes.

Captain Jackson: And my main problem there, or as far as Margaret Carrington was concerned, when I gave the birthdate of September, what date? I had to be 18 before a given date in September. Fortunately, I was 18 the first day of September, so I made it; otherwise, I would have had to wait another year. I would have gone to another school.

Paul Stillwell: How did you pick the specific nursing school you went to?

Captain Jackson: It was close; it had a long and very good reputation. The hospital itself had started out not as Miami Valley Hospital but as a Lutheran hospital put up by the clergy in Dayton for the care of the indigent sick and for the training of Lutheran deaconesses in nursing. And the setup there was--I don't know whether you know about Pastor Fliedner's nursing school in Germany, where he did this.[*]

Paul Stillwell: No.

Captain Jackson: Well, this was the beginning. Florence Nightingale went there, really.[†] He had set up, and I can't remember the town in Germany, but I'll look it up by the time I see you at home. Anyway, he had established the first school of nursing in the modern sense, let's say, where there was a planned curriculum, and it was for Lutheran deaconesses too. When this got to be such a burden that the Lutheran clergy could not support it, it was taken over by the Miami Valley Hospital Society, and the first director of nursing there was a graduate of Blockley, which is the Philadelphia General Hospital. And the director of that school, the first director of that school of nursing, had been a graduate of the Nightingale school in England.

---

[*] In the early 1850s Florence Nightingale attended Pastor Theodor Fliedner's Institution of Protestant Deaconneses at Kaiserswerth, Germany.
[†] Florence Nightingale (1820-1910) was an English nurse, reformer, and philanthropist. She gained prominence for a number of innovations introduced during the Crimean War in the 1850s.

So you see, we had a very fine tradition in quality in that school. And we had still, even with a part of the group that was no longer a religious school, but we still maintained a lot of it. For instance, you went to chapel before you went on duty in the morning. That was part of it. You were expected to look after, if you needed to, the spiritual background of people, to help them. And there were many frightened people in the hospital, you know. They're going up for surgery, and they're afraid. They're going into labor, and they're afraid. You can give them some reassurance. You have to understand them and find out, if you can, what their religious background is. If you know anything about it, you can help them.

And all of this was a part of a curriculum, even at that period, which was from 1927 to 1930.

Paul Stillwell: Was it the Lutheran denomination that it was affiliated with?

Captain Jackson: It had been, but it was not at the time I went there.

Paul Stillwell: I see.

Captain Jackson: That was a non-religious group. What it amounted to was that on the board were some of the more important business people, along with the people who worked for philanthropy and so on. It had a very fine board.

Paul Stillwell: Was it a non-denominational religious orientation?

Captain Jackson: Yes, it was completely non-denominational. We had St. Elizabeth's, which was the Catholic hospital there. They had a school of nursing but only two years. The nuns ran it, and I used to do some private duty over there after I graduated. I knew them, and, as I say, they had a good quality of patient care. Later they went into the three-year program, and then their course was accredited.

Paul Stillwell: What was included in the curriculum at your school?

Captain Jackson: Well, what was ordinarily the background. Somewhere in that mess of things that I've got there--my memory bank, which is all over the library--I think I have some of my report cards from school. But, of course, the principles of nursing was one of the very important things. Then we had medical, surgical, pediatric, communicable disease nursing. In other words, the things that you would naturally be confronted with in the care of patients.

So you had a probationary period, and I think that was either four or six months. That was a way that they simply did not get an individual who didn't qualify in academic or in your practical work. They simply did not carry you beyond the probationary period, and that gave the individual a chance to retain their dignity a little bit. They could say, "Well, I didn't like it, so I didn't stay on." And that didn't devastate them completely.

And, of course, they were guided away from something that they never would have been satisfied with anyway, because they didn't have that capacity and that temperament. And it gave the faculty long enough time to determine whether this individual had the kind of temperament that would go well in the world of nursing, meeting people in their times of stress. Because, believe me, you see people through some of the roughest times of their lives.

Paul Stillwell: I'm sure of that.

Captain Jackson: And having come from a home where I had a very happy life, it was easier for me because I had--when I say it was easier for me, I knew that people had tragedy. But I had a security that I could transmit to them, and it made a difference. It was very interesting, because, as a very young nurse, people would wait many times until I came on duty and then talk with me about the things they were worried about.

And, of course, if they needed some kind of counseling, I had been brought up in a family of very religious origin, you see, with a whale of a lot of ministers and what have you in it. And it was a growing part, not as much as it later became. And, of course, one of the criteria there was that you never betray a patient's confidence. Later on, we came into the business that the doctor and the nurse and so on ought to get together and try to analyze and see how they can help a patient, trade information.

That jolted me, and I told them at Columbia University, "You're betraying the confidence of the patient when you do that." There are ways that you can ask questions of a doctor without going into all of this specific thing in relation to that individual patient: "How would you suggest you meet a situation like this?" Let the doctor feel smart. He might have something that you didn't think of, you know. [Laughter]

Paul Stillwell: Did you have specific courses in counseling and medical ethics?

Captain Jackson: We had ethics definitely, nursing history and ethics, very definitely. And that was a part of it and it was very strict and very strictly taught and very strictly adhered to. That's what I was getting at, this business that you did not betray a patient's confidence.

Now, if it was something that had to do with the progress of their illness, then you told the doctor, but not if it was a family problem that they were worried about and they needed just to talk it out with somebody, that kind of thing. That you kept mum on. You didn't mention it to any other nurse, other than to say to them, briefly, I mean, she's worried about her children at home, not saying that she doesn't think her husband will take good care of them while she's gone, having this baby, you know. I mean, with this kind of thing, at least you've given them a clue.

We were all smart enough to put the tab mark under it and know probably what that concern was about. And if she spoke to the other one, well, that was their same situation, but you didn't pass it around between each other. You gave them all of the information that had to do with the well-being of that patient, as far as their illness was concerned, but you didn't parade their private life all over the place.

Paul Stillwell: Well, I think there's almost a parallel here with the military and classified information and the need to know.

Captain Jackson: Yes, that was it. I guess that was why I got an early top secret classification when I came back from Japan.* I had that almost immediately, because I could always keep my mouth shut. I like people, I like to talk with them, but things that were verboten were verboten.† Every now and then I get a German word in; I never learned the German language. My father was of German origin. That gives you a very brief background. In fact, I have all my textbooks there and everything in the library from my school of nursing. This is why I felt that if you wanted to come, you could see a lot more when--

Paul Stillwell: Sure.

Captain Jackson: What I'm doing right now is--three years I've been trying, yet, with an old house like that, they are gracious and they are beautiful to live in, but they require some maintenance too. It's brick, a ten-inch-thick wall. Every now and then some of that brickwork has to be replaced. When I bought it, I had a lot of work to do.

But, to get back to the fact of my grandmother, they decided that Leona would stay with her, and so I stayed the first year of high school. She was in much better health the next year.

Paul Stillwell: What year was that?

Captain Jackson: That was the 1923-24 school year. And that was the way the family handled things, don't you see. It was a Sunday dinner over at Grandma's, and all of the children were there. My Uncle Louie, who was the oldest, and his wife and family, and my father, who was the second one, and all of us, and Uncle Fred, who was the third one, and his wife and their family, and Aunt Dora and her family. Aunt Dora married that year. The next year my brother was born, and so was her oldest daughter; they were born just a couple of months from each other.

---

* As she relates later in the interview, Captain Jackson was captured on the island of Guam at the outset of World War II and subsequently repatriated to the United States after being held in captivity in Japan.
† "Verboten" is the German word for "forbidden."

So Aunt Dora said--well, they were still living on a farm. They had one of the old farmhouses of brick, you know, similar to the house that I have. There's still a lot of that. A lot of it's been torn down, but there's still a lot of those very gracious old houses around in that section of Ohio.

Where is your home state?

Paul Stillwell: Well, I was born in Dayton but I grew up in Missouri, so I have no recollections of Ohio.

Captain Jackson: Well, there is a similarity, though, in the area. But I don't know that much about Missouri.

Anyway, her proposal was that if I stayed with her, there were things that had to be done around the farm and so on. I could keep an eye on Bonnie, her baby, while they did the evening chores that had to be done: feeding the cattle and the milking, just the things that had to be done in a modern farm.

Well, it's always been a joke between Bonnie and me, and I said, "Bonnie, you should have had no difficulty becoming a teacher."

"Well," she said, "Why?"

I said, "Well, because I used to do my homework on the farm. You had three years of Latin, you had a semester of geometry, you had a year of physics, you had a year of chemistry, to say nothing of the English courses." I said, "I would recite them to you." I would get the supper ready, you know, while they were out. She'd be in her carriage or her playpen, and I'd go over my homework aloud to Bonnie. [Laughter] And so that's been a joke between her and me for all these years. [Laughter]

She, of course, did very well in college and I said, "I started you on your way, Bonnie."

Paul Stillwell: Some nursing schools are affiliated with colleges. Was that the case with Miami Valley?

Captain Jackson: Not at that point; not at that point. But in Ohio, we had one of the first university schools, up at Western Reserve. Frances Paine Bolton had endowed that school. And then, of course, later when I was on duty in Washington, I met Frances Paine Bolton and came to know her quite well. But that was the first one. Of course, I didn't even know about it at the time. I knew that Miami Valley was a well-accredited school and I knew people from there. Plus the fact that it was close enough to get home whenever I had time off.

Paul Stillwell: So all the courses were at the hospital itself?

Captain Jackson: Yes. Some were taught by doctors, some were taught by nurses. You see, you had pediatrics from an M.D., but you had pediatric nursing from a nurse. And the chief instructor was a graduate of University of Cincinnati. She was a graduate of Cincinnati General Hospital School of Nursing and then of the University of Cincinnati, so she had a baccalaureate degree. And we had some others who had baccalaureate degrees, but not all of the nursing people had it. They had had additional work, for instance, in a pediatric hospital, or something of the sort. And, of course, as far as medicine and surgery, we got a really fine background in our own hospital. And the evolution of the university schools of nursing, some of them had gone--well, Ohio State had one later, too, and some of the others. Some of the state universities developed schools on the collegiate level.

After World War II, I got in the fight toward the elevation of the basic nursing degree to the baccalaureate degree. I mean, we had a diploma of nursing--while I was the education officer in the Navy. But I'll go into that later.

You were asking about family background. And so, anyway, that illustrates the way the family still governed. It was a very interesting thing because, again, it was not unusual in that because my father was of a German origin family. His mother, as a matter of fact, was born in Germany. Her older brother and she were brought by their parents to America, I would say, around 1865, because she always said she was brought here when she was three and a half years old, and she was born in 1862. I've got the place at home that I can tell you the area of Germany that she was born in.

My grandfather's family was German, too, but they had come over earlier, about the 1840s, '30s to '40s, and of course, when my grandmother's family came, they had family here too. Her family was the Trost family, which is a German family. My father's family was the Class family, which is sometimes spelled K-L-A-S-S, sometimes K-L-A-U-S. In our instance, it was completely anglicized and spelled C-L-A-S-S.

My father's and my Uncle Louie's first language was German, so that they learned English when they went to school, and they learned it very precisely. My father had a very good command of English. And, of course, for years he was bilingual, but he didn't use the German very much. There had been World War I and then Hitler's rise to power.[*] At that particular time my father's hobby was shortwave radio, and, of course, he could pick up direct from Germany, and he followed Hitler through. And, of course, he didn't need somebody to translate. He knew colloquial German, and he knew some of the low Deutsch, too, which was over in the Belgian area. They have a language which is very closely related to German. But that he didn't try to keep up.

There were, however, a few people who were called German families who came from very close to that border, and their language was not completely high Deutsch. Now, we never learned it, because my mother didn't speak it. I think dad felt that it would put a wedge, she would feel it was a wedge, something that she didn't know about the development and growth of her daughters, you see, of her children. And I've always regretted it, because it would have been a handy thing to get it comfortably as you got English and to have known it at the time.

Anyway, after one of Hitler's rampages on the radio--this was much later. My son tells me that he watched his grandfather turn off the radio and say, "That man is crazy."

I said, "Well, he should have written to Neville Chamberlain and told him that."[†] [Laughter] I don't know whether Neville would have paid any attention to a small businessman, but, nonetheless, Dad would have a much better understanding about what

---

[*] Adolf Hitler was Chancellor of Germany from 1933 until his death in 1945.
[†] Neville Chamberlain served as Britain's Prime Minister from 1937 to 1940. He is best known for signing the Munich agreement with Germany's Adolf Hitler in late September 1938. He agreed to the partition of Czechoslovakia in return for a non-aggression pledge from Hitler. Chamberlain hailed the agreement as a guarantee of "peace in our time." Germany violated the pledge, and Britain declared war on Germany in September 1939.

Hitler was saying that anybody else, because I'm sure that Hitler did not speak anything more than a colloquial German.

But, of course, Dad had had school and, of course, there had been school in the family, too, so that he could have made himself understood anyplace in Germany.

Paul Stillwell: Well, I think Chamberlain was looking for an easy way out.

Captain Jackson: I think he was looking for an easy way out, and he fouled things up. I was on duty in Philadelphia at that particular time, and some of the girls were saying, "Oh, it's all over."

I said, "Are you out of your mind?" [Laughter] I've always been skeptical. I think I was born saying "Why?" I think that must have been the first word that I ever said. And they looked at me kind of strange, "Well, Chamberlain's going home."

I said, "That man isn't very smart."

"Well, why?"

I said, "You don't think for one minute that Hitler is going to stop anything because of the talk he's had with Chamberlain."

"Well, why not?"

I said, "Because Hitler has got completely distended ideas of his own importance, what Germany can do, and he's been training them to do it for quite a long time. There's been more than any of us know." And I said, "We still have German connections." We did. We had family that we heard from still. Now, we hadn't seen them, but there was still family there that kept a correspondence with people here. So the upshot of it was that Dad knew, and he kept all the way through. From that time on, he never missed anything, that there would be something in the paper that would tell him, or he'd just be cruising the German stations because he could get them.

So I had, from the beginning, a great deal of information about the situation in Europe, as far as the German end of it, from Hitler's propaganda, at least. And I was old enough at that time to think for myself, you know. I was a graduate nurse and had been for a while. And so the clan--as I said, we had sort of a clan relationship always in the family.

When it was something that was serious, they got together and made a decision, and nobody ever refused their decision. It occurred to me to say, I didn't want to stay with my grandparents. I loved them dearly. I had two sets of grandparents. My maternal grandmother died in 1918 in the influenza epidemic.[*] At that time I was about nine years old. I remember and I remember her very well, but I didn't have what it would have been to have grown up with her alive too. But there were things that she taught me that I have never forgotten.

And it was always a joke. Of course, we had horses and buggies at the time I was a little girl, still, and then we had a Maxwell. Later we had a Buick, and we went into the car generation. But they just were not available from the time I was small. Dad would harness the driving horse, and Mother would take Edythe, the sister next to me. It's spelled the Old English way, E-D-Y-T-H-E, because it's been in the family a while. Mother would take us over to the church, which had been founded by her great grandfather, and which most of the members of the family still belonged to.

Now, there was a church in our village, but she went over to her own church and, of course, that was a Sunday. She saw her parents, as long as my grandmother lived, and she saw my grandfather after that. She saw the cousins; they all went to the same church. That was the way to find out what was going on in the family, as well as going to church.

So it remained very close-knit, and I've always felt that I had the good fortune of being a little girl who had three sets of parents who loved me, but who never interfered with each other. There never was one word of criticism of my mother and father. Now, my Grandmother Class was inclined to make a comment sometimes, but not the rest of them. We were their children, and they were willing to share us with them. My grandfather used to come over with his horse-drawn buggy, and he would say, "Now, your mother told me not to come home without the girls."

So the girls would get a basket filled with their clean clothes, you know, and we'd go back with Grandpa and we'd get into the lane that led up to the house. And he'd say,

---

[*] In the worldwide influenza epidemic of 1918-19 some 20 million people died, including more than 500,000 in the United States.

"Now, you girls get down, and we'll surprise Grandma." So we'd get down in the buggy, and he'd drive into the driveway to the barn. And then he'd go, "Now, you be real quiet."

So we would go to the door with him. He'd knock on the door, and we'd hide behind the door as it opened, and then we'd yell, "Surprise" at Grandma. It was a game we played every time we went over there. You can begin to see the kind of childhood I had. It was a protected one, and yet I was taught responsibility, that you didn't blame other people when you did things you shouldn't do, that you were responsible for your own conduct. I got that pretty early in my life.

Paul Stillwell: When and where did you begin to practice nursing after you had gotten your degree?

Captain Jackson: In Dayton. I worked for quite a while with the Stillwater Sanitarium with tuberculosis patients, because tuberculosis was rampant. I am worried now on this whole business of boarding up and the energy-saving programs, where they've got houses so tightly insulated and so on they get no fresh air. Now, I went through an era when we tried to get people not to nail down the lower sash of their windows so they couldn't be opened during the winter, to the place where they'd open their windows and leave them open a little bit to get some fresh air, because tuberculosis was a very serious problem. One of these days I'm going to get around to write to the people in Atlanta and find out if they have any data in relation to the prevalence of tuberculosis now.* Has there been an increase?

I worked, as I say, for quite a while, a couple of years in that.

Paul Stillwell: Well, with all the pollution there is, I wonder if there's any longer any such thing as fresh air.

Captain Jackson: Well, I know. But you can rebreathe. If you had an illness, if you had bacteria of any kind, you know, you can rebreathe them and get all kinds of chest illnesses.

---

* The Centers for Disease Control and Prevention, located in Atlanta, Georgia, is an agency of the U.S. Government's Department of Health and Human Services.

Paul Stillwell: Did you have any long-term career plans that early, when you were in Dayton?

Captain Jackson: No, I didn't have that early career plans. I married. The marriage didn't turn out well.

Paul Stillwell: When were you married?

Captain Jackson: When I was 22, and then the divorce was shortly before I came into the Navy. And I had custody of my son because for two reasons. I didn't believe in the business of competing for a child. Now, I never said that he couldn't see his father or his father couldn't see him. And to this day, I have never said one word against his father to him. It just was not my way. When I came into the Navy, I left him with my parents. I knew that I had had a good childhood with them, and I thought he'd get a good childhood, and when he was old enough, I would take him with me. He was three and a half years old at that time.

And, of course, I could not take him with me, but to give my mother credit, she never let him forget that he had a mother. Of course, I compensated her for his care, and I took care of all his needs, plus the fact that I came home whenever I could. I also arranged for Mother to visit me. They were worried to lose their daughter into the Navy. Where all would she be going? So I invited her one year, and she brought Bob to the hospital in Philadelphia. They stayed in the nurses' quarters. They could meet the people that were my friends, that I was associated with. The chief nurse was very gracious; she was a very fine woman anyway. And mother went home completely satisfied that if this was what I wanted, this was what she wanted.

Then the year that the World Fair was in Brooklyn, in 1939--that year was Dad's turn to come. I've been trying to remember the name of that hotel in Brooklyn that everybody stayed at. It was not too far from the hospital, and it was quite a good hotel and in the better part of Brooklyn. And, of course, the subways came in; there was a subway station in the base of it.

Anyway, I put Dad up over there, and then I took him over to the fair. If I remember, that was on Long Island, wasn't it?

Paul Stillwell: Yes, in Flushing Meadows.

Captain Jackson: Flushing Meadows, yes, and I took him over and then, of course, I couldn't go every day. So once he had been over, then I wrote down the subways that he was to take, the transportation, so he could go every day. And he had the time of his life.

Paul Stillwell: What year was your son born?

Captain Jackson: In '32.

Paul Stillwell: Okay, so he was seven years old by the time of the fair.

Captain Jackson: Yes.

Paul Stillwell: What led to your being interested in the Navy?

Captain Jackson: Wright-Patterson Air Force Base was not Wright-Patterson Air Force Base at that time.*

Paul Stillwell: Wright Field.

Captain Jackson: It was Wright Field. It was Fairfield Air Depot and Patterson Field. Now, remember, there was no Air Force at that time.† The Army had no hospital; they had

---

* Wright-Patterson Air Force Base is located near Dayton, Ohio.
† On 20 June 1941 the U.S. Army Air Corps was officially redesignated the U.S. Army Air Forces. In 1947 the designation was changed again, this time to the current title, U.S. Air Force.

a dispensary but no hospital, and anybody who required hospital care came to Miami Valley. I had a first lieutenant in the Army Air Corps as a patient on one of the floors where I worked at Miami Valley. One evening his wife stayed over. I was on night duty at that particular time. She stayed over so that we could meet, and we became very close friends, Frances and I. He told me about her, you know, and about what it was like over there. Frances was surprised, because she said her husband was ordinarily rather a reserved kind of person, but he could talk comfortably with me.

Well, one weekend I was out to their quarters spending the weekend with them, and Frances and I were standing before a mirror about the size of that one. Each of us was putting on lipstick; we were going down to the club for dinner. And in the middle of putting lipstick on, we both kind of looked at each other, and I said, "Do you see what I see?"

And she said, "Yes." We looked more alike than my sisters looked like me.

I said, "That's why Clarence can talk comfortably to me. I look like some of your family." [Laughter] And that was a long-term friendship.

And somehow or another somebody was doing something that I considered stupid at the hospital. I was a little out of humor, and Clarence said, "Well, why don't you try the Army Nurse Corps." He said, "That is a pretty good situation." And then he said, "Or maybe the Navy. They're in good cities; they're not all back in some cornfield like the Army stations are."

I thought, "Well, now, why don't I look into that?" So I did. I wrote to both groups, and the Army's requirements were that you be 5-foot-2, and I wasn't quite 5-foot-2. The Navy was mainly interested in what you could do professionally. As long you were in good health, they had no restraints as to the fact that you weren't quite as tall as somebody else. So I wound up making my application to the Navy, and I was accepted without any question. And they asked about Bob, and I sent them a copy of my divorce decree. I told them that under any circumstances my parents would be taking care of my son, whether I was there or not, and that later on, he would be with me, but he would be in perfectly good hands. After all, they brought me up, and I hadn't done too badly, so I was quite sure I could trust them with him.

Paul Stillwell: How large was the Navy's Nurse Corps at that time?

Captain Jackson: Before the war, we had 400 nurses. In fact, I had as many on Guam, when I went out the second time, as we had had in the whole Nurse Corps when I came in.[*]

Paul Stillwell: Did they have rather stringent admission requirements?

Captain Jackson: Very. You had to have at least two years' experience. I had six years, which made a difference. They were glad to get somebody with that kind of background. At the time of my application, I had left Stillwater, and I had gone back to Miami Valley. I had gone on staff to begin with, and they had just asked me to take one of the private floors as head nurse. I had had that about three weeks when the Navy's acceptance came through.

So I went into the Navy, and it proved to be exactly what I wanted. It had the amount of discipline, it had the quality of care. I had, within the hospital situation, a working relationship with doctors that I had never had in another hospital, because they were stationed there. One of the doctors that I worked with on his ward for ten months was a man who later was Surgeon General and who nominated me for director of the Nurse Corps.[†]

Paul Stillwell: Who was that?

Captain Jackson: Lamont Pugh.[‡] The situation in the Navy was that you could talk with a doctor as a professional colleague. There was one nurse on the floor. Your people who did the care were the hospital corpsmen. You got them from the hospital corps school. But when I used a young hospital corpsman with a sick patient, I worked with that

---

[*] As later sections of the oral history relate, Jackson was captured by the Japanese on Guam in December 1941 and subsequently came back to the United States in the summer of 1942. In December 1944 she returned to Guam after it had been recaptured by U.S. forces.

[†] As a captain, Leona Jackson served as director of the Navy Nurse Corps from 1954 to 1958.

[‡] Rear Admiral Herbert Lamont Pugh, MC, USN, served as the Navy's Surgeon General from 1951 to 1955.

corpsman on that patient to be very sure that he knew how to handle that sick patient. And, of course, he didn't have those kind of sick patients in corps school. That was further teaching, don't you see.

I used to say to them, jokingly, "Now, one of these days you're going to be out someplace on a forward line, and you're going to have to do something, and you're going to wonder if I don't teach you now. I'm not going to be at your elbow to tell you what to do, you know, so you better learn it now." And you'd be surprised how many of them told me after the war that they had thought of that when they were with the Marines. [Laughter]

But, I mean, this was the way you handled it. Now, the ward that he had--remember that we did not have any antibiotics. We did not have sulfa in '36, when I went into the Navy. We began using sulfa, and I don't remember exactly the year, but it was new in that '36 to '39 period. And the surgical patients were all outside the ward; the surgical patients were separated. If there was any suggestion of an infection, they went to one ward and on the other ward only clean surgery--no ruptured gallbladders, no ruptured appendixes or anything of that kind on that ward, because with the best technique in the world, a hospital is a place where you can transmit bacteria from one patient to another one.

Paul Stillwell: Of course.

Captain Jackson: So Dr. Pugh had what we called them, to ourselves, clean and dirty surgery.* Dr. Pugh had dirty surgery, which meant that we had a high proportion of very sick patients. He was a University of Virginia graduate, and that is an excellent medical school. Some of the finest doctors I knew were graduates of that school. But we had, as a general rule, very, very good doctors in those years in the Navy, and I worked closely with them.

Dr. Pugh would come down on the ward after the surgery, and he would sit down at the desk. We'd sit down side by side, and we'd go over the patients who had been operated. He would tell me exactly what he'd done. Well, I had had operating room experience as a

---

* In the late 1930s, when he was stationed at the Philadelphia Naval Hospital, Pugh was a lieutenant in the Navy Medical Corps.

student nurse, you see, as a part of my program--three months of it, as a matter of fact. That was required by the Ohio state board, and so I knew what he was talking about. I'd been through those things before, and he would tell me what he thought the prognosis was and what might come up. If we'd had a similar case, I would say to him, "Well, now, Dr. Pugh, with So-and-so, you did it this way. What's the difference?"

Now, he knew I wasn't questioning his ability. I was trying to learn, so if that problem hit me when he wasn't there, I'd know the immediate steps to take, and he knew that was the way.

Paul Stillwell: You said that you were treated as a professional colleague. Had that not been the case in civilian nursing?

Captain Jackson: You were always--the doctors came and went. That was the way it was. Yes, you were treated--but I never had a doctor sit down at the desk and go over his patients with me. But in the Navy it did.

Paul Stillwell: Were civilian nurses more looked down on? Would that be a fair statement?

Captain Jackson: No, not that. The doctor wrote the orders, and he presumed you'd follow the orders, and that was it. Well, in the Navy, they recognized you as a professional colleague, and you could ask questions. And I did always. It was amazing how many of the doctors kept in touch with me. When the war broke out, I used to hear from some of them every now and then.

He would go over every step of that operation and exactly what he had found. So then he knew that if an emergency came up--and it did sometimes--he might be scrubbed up in the operating room with a patient on the table in process of surgery; he couldn't come down then. So I had to be there to give that information to whoever was the officer of the day. If I had all that information, the OOD could move in and handle that patient until Dr. Pugh could get down from the operating room, which gave a much greater margin of safety in the patient care than otherwise would have prevailed.

It had one adverse effect. The word got around among the residents that if you went onto Dr. Pugh's ward and Mrs. Jackson suggested that this was the way Dr. Pugh would handle that patient, you'd better handle it that way. Because if you didn't, you'd hear from Dr. Pugh when he got down from the operating room.

Paul Stillwell: Well, so he'd obviously developed a good deal of confidence in you.

Captain Jackson: Well, but you could work that way when you worked together. And he knew that if I gave him a report on a patient, that I'd looked that patient over pretty carefully and that there wasn't any question. If he wanted to know what the patient's blood pressure was, I had it ready. I mean, I had checked that blood pressure before I called him and this kind of thing. It was a way of working together in this kind of a professional arrangement because you supplemented each other.

Paul Stillwell: What might be an example of one of those emergencies that he couldn't attend to right away?

Captain Jackson: Well, you might get a patient who would start to bleed or something of that kind. You could put pressure dressings on if it wasn't too bad. But I would not have taken the responsibility of just putting a pressure dressing on and left it without having a doctor see the patient, don't you see. In the meantime, I'd let Dr. Pugh know about it.

Paul Stillwell: So the officer of the day was a doctor?

Captain Jackson: Oh, yes, he was a medical officer. He might not be of the same specialty, but he had a background. Remember that they all had got their M.D., and then they went on to specialize in whatever field they were in. Now, not all had specialized; some of them were general practitioners, but they had enough of the background to know what this implied.

If there was anything beyond what I had done, he could handle it until such time as Dr. Pugh could get down. Now, what he would do would be finish the operation that he had, but not have the next one brought up right on schedule, don't you see. And I would say, "Bring the patient up to the operating room." You know, we're talking about getting some bleeding or something. Or he'd come down, and all it would do would be delay his schedule a little bit. But in the meantime I had had somebody else who had had more background in medicine than I had to look at the patient. So everything had been done to give that patient the best care that could be made available, and it was pretty darn good.

It's amazing, when you have been in nursing for a while, how you can almost immediately or instinctively know when something isn't going well. Our wards in Philadelphia and in Brooklyn--in Brooklyn my surgical service was two wards with a capacity for 99 patients. And there was one nurse for that, plus the hospital corpsman. So what would happen is that you simply kept everything under control. I could sit in the middle of that ward, if I was on afternoon duty--after lights out, I could sit in the middle of that ward at my desk writing out my reports and so on. If a patient coughed, I knew who that patient was. You get that kind of sensitivity to it, and you get an instinct about patients.

I know one night I was on night duty. And I had had that medical ward. There was a Veterans Administration patient, because before World War II the Veterans Administration did not have the complex of hospitals that they have now. The naval hospitals and the Army hospitals took them in, because it gave us a wider spectrum of patients, you see. Our patients were mainly of the active duty age, and at that point we did not have facilities for wives and children. So that you had a narrowed spectrum of patients. Well, if you took on the Veterans Administration patients, you got this other end of the spectrum. So you kept your hand in pretty well in general medicine and general nursing.

This man was a veteran, who was a cardiac patient and had been on the critical list for a long time. The critical list meant that anything could happen with a patient. Everything was being done, but they were very seriously ill. On night duty, we tried to make rounds every hour. Now, in Philadelphia, there were two night nurses. I had four floors, and then the rest of it would be on the other night nurse. There would be a night nurse up in the sick officers' quarters who would take the floors down and I would take them up. I made rounds that night, and, somehow or other, when I took a look at that man, I thought there was something wrong. He did not look well. I checked pulse, I checked blood pressure--all the normal signs--and they hadn't changed any, but <u>he</u> had changed.

Well, I called the officer of the day, and the officer of the day was an orthopedic surgeon that I had worked with, too, and I said, "Dr. Kreuz, I cannot put my finger on it, but there is something wrong with this man. He's not good."[*]

Well, he got out his stethoscope and did as much of an examination that he could do without disturbing the patient too much, I mean, enough to know. He said, "I can't find anything."

I said, "Well, I couldn't either, but he just does not look well. There's a change; there's a definite change there. I cannot put my finger on it. I can't tell you what it is. But at least we've checked all of the vital symptoms and there doesn't appear to be anything that we can do more than is already being done."

But when I went off duty that morning, I said to the chief nurse, I said, "That man is going to die. That is my feeling." I said, "We have checked. Dr. Kreuz checked him thoroughly, chest, abdomen, you know, the whole thing." And I said, "I had checked pulse, blood pressure, TPRs, the whole works, respiration, the whole works. Neither of us could find a change.[†] We looked on the chart and here was the same thing charted."

Well, I got up to take a shower in the shower room around 3:00 o'clock that afternoon, and the day nurse came into the bathroom at the same time I was there. And she said, "Guess what?"

I said, "What do you mean?"

She said, "So-and-so died today."

I said, "What time?"

She said, "About noon."

I said, "I told Miss Lambert that this morning. I couldn't put my finger on it. I had the OOD see him. We were doing everything that could possibly be done for him." But I

---

[*] Lieutenant (junior grade) Frank P. Kreuz, Jr., MC, USN, stationed at Philadelphia in the late 1930s.
[†] TPRs--temperature, pressure, respiration. The current term used in place of TPR is "vital signs."

had that instinct. There was something about that man that told me, and I had kept a very close watch on him for the rest of the night. I didn't stay in that--well, for a while I stayed in that ward after I had made ward rounds. In other words, what I did was I made ward rounds, and I made that the last ward, and then anything that I had left out of the hour before I had to start rounds again I'd spend in that ward.

Paul Stillwell: So you were looking for something overt.

Captain Jackson: Yes. But I couldn't find anything overt. What happened was that he just wore out. We knew he would, because he had had this heart damage, apparently from his World War I experiences. Anyway, this is why I say that we did not have, at that time, the monitoring systems that they have now. You had to develop and trust your own monitoring system on patients. If you could pick them up quick enough, you could save them. And, of course, I had been trying to pick them up a little longer than some of the other people had.

I mean, this gives a little idea of what nursing was like.

Paul Stillwell: Sure. Was there any specific orientation program on Navy-type things after you joined.

Captain Jackson: Well, not at that time, but the way it was handled was that you were assigned to work with a senior nurse. She taught you what the procedures were in the hospital and how you managed to get things. It was during World War II that we set up the orientation programs in two, I believe, it was two centers in the Nurse Corps. The WAVES had theirs set up at one of the women's colleges.*

After the war we merged the orientation centers, and the nurses and the WAVES were assigned to the same place. Of course, the nurses wore a different uniform during the war than the WAVES did. But after the end of the war, we all decided we'd take the

---

* WAVES--Women accepted for Voluntary Emergency Service. The WAVES had a training program at Smith College, Northampton, Massachusetts. The Naval Institute collection contains two volumes of recollections from World War II women naval officers.

Mainbocher WAVE uniform.* I have pictures that I will show you when you come to visit me of myself in uniform. They don't have anything over in Navy archives, and I'm reluctant to send them, because it would look like I'm a little egotistical, but unfortunately I don't have anybody else in uniform. My sister was a Navy nurse, but I don't have any of her pictures.

But we were distinguished from the WAVES by the uniform. On our uniform the coat was very much like the men's, double-breasted with a blue skirt and a different hat, not that hat that they wear now.

Paul Stillwell: Well, the Navy nurses' hat in World War II was almost like a beret, wasn't it?

Captain Jackson: Yes. It was the top of an officer's hat and then, as I say, the uniforms changed. And the white ones, of course, had the epaulets on the shoulders. I have a very good picture that Harris and Ewing did here.† I was proud of being in uniform, you know, when I got back to the United States. Of course, we wore hospital uniforms but not the regular Navy uniform before the beginning of World War II. But once we got back, we were in uniform like everybody else. And then, of course, at the end of the war, we didn't have to wear them off duty.

Paul Stillwell: How did your initial assignment to Philadelphia come about?

Captain Jackson: It was the closest to my home; I didn't ask for it. Also, it was one of the new and beautiful hospitals in the Navy.‡ And the reason for that, too, was it saved transportation money, you see, because I was not very far away. Also, it was to my advantage because I could get home, not for long periods of time. I traveled it some many times, that railroad train that I used to go through. You picked it up in Washington, and it took on some little cars in Pittsburgh, and then you came on west. At Pittsburgh, some of

---

* In 1942, Mainbocher, a noted American designer, developed a uniform for the WAVES that was so well accepted that it has remained in use by Navy women for many years.
† Harris and Ewing was the name of a prominent Washington, D.C., photo studio.
‡ The Philadelphia Naval Hospital had been commissioned in 1935.

them went on to Chicago, and some went down to St. Louis. It was the St. Louis something or other, and it was on for years and years. When they took that railroad off, I certainly missed it because I had made so many trips. It was a night trip, and it meant when I came off duty, I could catch the night trip, you see, and be at home in the morning.

Paul Stillwell: How frequently did you go back to Ohio?

Captain Jackson: Well, of course, I went back on leave and when I had a weekend sometimes I'd go back. Your weekend usually would be Saturday afternoon and Sunday. I mean, you would have it off, but ordinarily you worked Saturday afternoon or Sunday afternoon. You alternated, but every now and then you would have a weekend, which would give you a day and a half, and that meant that I could pick up the Saturday evening train and get home on Sunday and then leave Sunday night and come back to Philadelphia.

But we've certainly rambled over a lot of things. Are there things that particularly . . . ?

Paul Stillwell: Did you have quarters there at the navy yard in Philadelphia?

Captain Jackson: No, the nurses' quarters were on the hospital compound. They were very nice quarters.

Paul Stillwell: Where was the hospital located in relation to the navy yard?

Captain Jackson: It was just up Broad Street from the navy yard. I loved Philadelphia. There were many interesting things there. I decided when I went to Philadelphia that I was going to find out something about the city. I was going to learn my way around in it. So whenever I had an afternoon off, I would get the bus that stopped in front of our compound and take myself up to the center of Philadelphia and then pick up the trolley or bus or whatever it was to an area of the city or the suburbs that I hadn't seen before. I would go on that bus to the end and then take another bus back. I had seen it. If I wanted to get off and look, I did. If it looked like it was kind of sleazy, I didn't get off. I just waited until it came around or another one was going the other way.

I did the same thing in New York. I think I've been on practically every subway in New York, the elevated, and the what have you. I'd go over from Brooklyn, and I learned New York very well. The streetcar came by the quarters; we had to walk out, of course, onto the street, but there was a stop there. Then you came over to Wall Street and picked up the subway.

And, of course, then, when I was in Brooklyn, I traveled a good bit, because I went to other schools. I was brought up, I guess, with a respect for knowledge, and the approach to knowledge was a school. In fact, the first school in Miami County was in the living room of Joseph Furniss, who was the first of the Furniss family born in the colonies, and that was where he taught children to read and write and some basic arithmetic and so on. And to this day, when I want to know anything, I enroll for a course.

For instance, I decided that it was time that I got acquainted with computers, find out what it was all about. So there's a joint vocational school very close to where I live. They have Saturday morning classes, and they have other classes. Well, I looked in their flyer, and they had some things on computers. So I called, just a little bit before all this happened.

Paul Stillwell: You mean with your eyes.

Captain Jackson: Yes, and I was too late to get the arrangement that they had, but they were going to have another one in the summer and I said to them, "Now, I don't intend to be a computer technician or anything like that. I just want to know what it can do and how it fits, whether it fits into my lifestyle nowadays." And so they told me about this, and what I fully intended to do was enroll for the course and find out how computers fit into the social pattern. I couldn't do it at the time, when their summer program began, because my vision wasn't good enough at that point.

But I think that it has improved some, even in the right eye. The left eye is completely absorbed, the hemorrhage. But, of course, I've still got the cataract process to go through, but once the cataract is off, it ought to restore my left eye to pretty good vision. But there are times when it blurs. So, anyway, I'll get around to it. As I told you, I had my 77th birthday, but that doesn't mean that I can't still learn something. I don't know all the things in the world. I've had a lot of experiences, but there are some I still haven't had. [Laughter]

Paul Stillwell: Did the Navy provide any additional training while you were in the hospital in Philadelphia? Was there a regular program?

Captain Jackson: No, no, other than the orientation, because, you see, I came in with a better background than most of the people. At the time, their requirement was two years' experience; well, I had six. So I found myself in a situation which I enjoyed. I've always enjoyed a challenge. When I found myself on a ward where they were having difficulties, I'd get that ward. I know we had an orthopedic ward there that they'd been having trouble with. The chief nurse came one day, and she said, "Well, the nurses can't seem to get along there. They've got a patient that seems to give them trouble [one of the Veterans Administration]. They all can't get along with Dr. Kreuz."

Well, Dr. Kreuz--that name was German, you know, and he was one of those direct-speaking kind of people. Well, I'd met them before, and so I went over onto the ward, and they said, well, they had one patient who was a Veterans Administration patient; he made a lot of trouble. Well, I just took things in stride, went over, and found out about Dr. Kreuz and how he handled his patients and what he wanted done. One of the things was that he wanted to see X-rays. So when he made rounds, any new X-rays were on the patient's bed. And they did not write their orders. You went with them on rounds with your order book, and they gave you verbal orders, and you wrote the verbal order down. When you finished your rounds, they reviewed it and signed it, and those were your orders, instead of writing orders on every chart.

Paul Stillwell: So that protected you.

Captain Jackson: Yes. And so it was no difficulty getting ready for his rounds. It was what I would consider a professional approach, and so then we were working one day for a field day. It was not too long after I came onto the ward and the Veterans Administration man, who was supposed to have been the source of all the trouble--you see, for field day, everything would be done. Beds would be washed once a week. There were never any cleaner hospitals than any naval hospitals, believe me, and everything was spic and span for a white-glove inspection, if they wanted to use it that way.

Your ambulatory patients that would not come to any harm, you would put them to minor chores that were within their capacity, as well as your hospital corpsmen. Well, I had a senior hospital corpsman who would go to the patients and ask them to help. I looked up, and so help me, here was this man who was supposed to be the trouble-maker. He was washing beds for all he was worth, and nobody had asked him. I said to this senior corpsman, "How did you get that?"

He said, "I don't know, he just got up and did it."

There were several others of the patient who had volunteered to help, and I said, "This is the workingest ward I have ever seen." And the man's name was Jackson. He was intrigued by the fact that the head nurse's name was Jackson too.

He said, "Well, you know why?"

I said, "No."

He said, "You don't nag at me."

I said, "Well, why should I nag at you when you're so good without it?" [Laughter]

Well, that welded the relationship. He was my shadow from that day on, and we never had the slightest trouble with him after that. It was the same kind of situation that you run into in any place where you have people with varying degrees of experience. I know that the chief master-at-arms who assigned the corpsmen to the wards soon got onto that. I had a first-class pharmacist's mate come onto my ward as senior corpsman. It was very unusual to get a first class on a ward. He was usually put in some of the technical areas or something of that kind. Haas came on the ward and said to me, "I have not been in a hospital for quite a while. I've been with the Marine Corps. There are a lot of things I don't know."

I said, "Haas, that's fine. You let me know when you don't know, and I'll help you." If you had not been in a hospital situation, but with the Marine Detachments, I would expect that there were things in a hospital that were new to you." And I said, "You just let me know, and I'm sure we'll get along fine." And we did. Well, this word got around that Haas was a pretty good senior corpsman.

Up in the venereal disease ward, the night nurse made rounds to be sure that everything was all right. But those people were up and about, so you didn't need a nurse up there all the time. So usually there was a senior corpsman up there who looked after the treatments and so on. Once I was in the elevator with the urologist, and he said to me, "I understand that Haas is a pretty good corpsman."

I said, "Yes, he is, he's fine." And I thought, well, Haas, you're on your way to the sixth floor. So the chief came up kind of apologetic and said, "I'd like to send Haas up to Dr.--" I can't remember the man's name; I can see him as plain as anything.

I said, "Well, that's fine. He can handle it. He's perfectly capable. He came in to me and said he didn't know it all, and we worked together and he knows it now. You will have no trouble there." So he sent me another corpsman, Cooper, who had come on a few days before that. I said, "Incidentally, the man you sent me is quite good."

He kind of smiled, and he said, "You know something?"

I said, "No, now what are you up to?"

He said, "He's had trouble with some of the other nurses in the ward." He said, "I sent him up for you to find out what is the matter."

I said, "Well, where have you had him?" He gave me the ward number, and I said, "Well, now, the nurse who is on that ward, I know her. She came to me for orientation." I said, "She's an excellent nurse, but she hasn't been here long enough yet to be secure in her position. She is afraid that she will not stand up to what I taught her or that she'll do something wrong at this point. You need to send him to a more experienced nurse and you did." So I said, "He is fine."

And he said, "Well, then I'll leave him a senior corpsman."

I said, "That suits me fine, and it will suit Cooper"

So it worked out. This is what I'm saying, you've got a whole tier of people with varying experiences, and you're going to have differences in the way they get along and differences in the way things operate. But it can be remedied if you know what you're doing.

Paul Stillwell: Are you using the term pharmacist's mate and hospital corpsman interchangeably?

Captain Jackson: You had hospital corpsman first class and second class, and then you had pharmacist's mate third class, second class, first class. They were the hospital corpsmen as they moved up their rates.

Paul Stillwell: Well, that term pharmacist's mate is no longer used. Now it's just hospital corpsman.

Captain Jackson: Yes, I know they've changed much of it.* I'm giving it to you as it was at that time. Of course, we're talking about a different era, and much of that was changed after World War II, because, you see, the whole structure of the hospital corps and the Medical Service Corps changed in World War II. There was a great deal of need for pathologists, for the scientists of various medical scientists who were not M.Ds, don't you see, but who could handle the laboratory work and other things that were coming into use. The Medical Service Corps used to be the steps that a hospital corpsman could finally take to commissioned status if he qualified.†

Well, having these people come in with Ph.Ds to start out with, you put a great deal of competition to the career hospital corpsman, and so they made the differential in terms of the science group. But a hospital corpsman who had worked all of a career to get to the place where he might be named as chief of the hospital corps could easily be displaced as chief of a hospital by a Ph.D. Well, there was a bad feeling there, as there would naturally

---

* From 1916 to 1948 the enlisted rating was known as pharmacist's mate. From 1948 to the present the rating has been titled hospital corpsman.
† Some hospital corpsmen still follow this path to commissioned officer status.

be, because part of his opportunity that he worked for was gone. It was the same situation I saw in the State Department where your Foreign Service officers worked to get up here, and a political appointee was made the ambassador.

Paul Stillwell: I understand that. Well, I think what you're saying is that in the Medical Service Corps they were aspiring to handle the administrative end.

Captain Jackson: That's right, that's right, because the scientists who came in knew nothing about the administration of a hospital. They had their laboratories or whatever it was, and that's where they functioned. So it took a lot of sorting out and a lot of technique and a lot of tact to work it out. I know that when I was director of the Nurse Corps, they had in charge of the hospital corps, under the Medical Service Corps, a man who had come up the ranks. When he got into trouble, he'd come to me, not to the head of the Medical Service Corps. He'd come to me, and I'd help him unwind it.

I know there was a question that came up about when BuPers wanted to assign hospital corpsman.[*] The hospital corps itself had been assigning them. Well, it happened that they had been revising the manual of the medical department. I had assigned my assistant to that, and she was a very experienced nurse with her baccalaureate from Columbia and a very, very fine person. Hazel and I worked very closely together, and I said, "Take any of the other staff. Get the help of any of them and come through with this, because there are things in that medical department that prevent nurses from functioning as effectively as they can." I said, "The hospital corps and Medical Service Corps have always been in charge of the hospital corps. But they do a great deal of the nursing work, and the nurses are responsible for the nursing. So I think we should get into this a section that says that the duty assignments of the hospital corps will be subject to the approval of the Nurse Corps."

Now, I didn't mean the Nurse Corps in Washington, but I meant on duty, don't you see. Well, what happened was that BuPers was going to take away the hospital corps's

---

[*] BuPers--Bureau of Naval Personnel.

authority to assign their own people to the hospitals or dispensaries or wherever it was. So he came to me, and he was very upset. And I said, "Okay, I'll handle it."

So called BuPers, and I identified myself and I said, "Look, I think you're getting into a little trouble here."

"Well, what about it?"

I said, "Well, the manual of the medical department has been approved, and it says that the assignment of hospital corpsmen is subject to approval of the Nurse Corps."

And he said, "How come?"

I said, "Well, now look, you have no knowledge of the performance of these men."

"Well," he said, "we've got the fitness reports."

I said, "Sometimes those fitness reports aren't worth a darn." And I said, "If you're assigning somebody because of the length of time they've been in service and so on, into a dispensary or a place where they hadn't any nursing supervision, that may be the worst person you can put there. But the hospital corps and the Nurse Corps knows their performance, and we are responsible for the nursing care of patients. And I'm not willing to have somebody who's mediocre put into a place where they are the only corpsman."

Paul Stillwell: Did you have some sort of fitness report independent of the official one?

Captain Jackson: No.

Paul Stillwell: Was it just the reputation of individuals?

Captain Jackson: Well, the fitness report would be written by the hospital corps people, not by the nurses, don't you see.

Paul Stillwell: So the nurses knew them by reputation.

Captain Jackson: They knew them by having had them on their wards. And I said, "A man who deserved an appointment like that may not get it. But we know those people, because we work with them every day." So they backed down. [Laughter]

Paul Stillwell: Now, you mentioned this fellow Haas, who came from duty with the Marines. What sort of things would he have been deficient in in working in a hospital?

Captain Jackson: In the patient care, bed care. You see, what he would have been doing is working with inoculations, with the kind of injuries that might be happening on bivouac or something of that kind. But it was different when it came to a surgical ward, ordinarily with your most serious ill surgical patients in the hospital, because this was the infected surgery, dirty surgery ward. And there were new techniques in surgery. It was during that period of time, while I was on Dr. Kreuz's ward, that we started using the sulfa drugs. Well, now, sulfa drugs were completely new to him.

Paul Stillwell: What kind of difference did that make for you?

Captain Jackson: It made a tremendous difference. A lot of people came home alive. You see, the corpsmen could carry that. They could put the powdered sulfa into a wound immediately, which meant that you were beginning treatment of that patient as soon as somebody could get to him.

Paul Stillwell: Was this a forerunner to antibiotics?

Captain Jackson: No, the antibiotics are quite different. They were coming along, but they were not developed sufficiently to be used much in World War II. But you could take sulfa to the forward area, and the hospital corpsmen, if they survived the assault, could take care of the wounds around them immediately. That helped the odds in the favor of the patient.

Paul Stillwell: Was its value in preventing infection?

Captain Jackson: Yes. So, I mean, I went over that; I had a procedure always. If we got a new drug on the ward, a drug that we had not used there with a patient before, my corpsmen were lined up right around my desk. I went over the whole thing and told them what to give, what was the range of dosage. If they saw a dosage on either side of that, it was wrong, so they should come to me. I told them not, for heaven's sake, to take that kind of an order. Because the officer of the day, not being familiar with the patients, wouldn't necessarily order something like that, but there could be a mistake somewhere along the line. I wanted to take every practice we could that would prevent mistakes.

Also, I would tell them what the side effects would be, what to expect, and so on. I remember one time, it was when I introduced sulfa on the orthopedic ward. We had a Marine who was in a body cast. He had been in that cast for a good while, and he had some infections. Dr. Kreuz ordered the sulfa, and that was the first time I administered it.

Well, I read the whole pamphlet, and then I called everybody together and gave them the background on it. Several hours later, one of the corpsman came to me very excited and he said, "Miss Jackson, So-and-so is bleeding."

I said, "What do you mean, bleeding?"

"Well, he has blood in his urine."

I said, "Oh, for God's sake, I forgot to tell you, it's a dye. Let me see it." The minute I took one look at it, I said, "That's the sulfa. I forgot to tell you that it's excreted through the urine and it has a color." But I said, "Thank you. Now I know I can trust you. You do listen and you do watch." [Laughter] But that was the only time I ever fouled up on it.

But, anyway, I had worked long enough with those young men that they knew when I said this is the way it will be, that that was the way it was to be, because it was the best for all concerned. When we were talking over the phone, you said you thought I was pretty strict. Well, I am. As I told you, as far as patient care was concerned, I was very strict.

But the whole thing of it was that this was a way of keeping them up, and these were the things that Haas didn't know. He didn't know the new drugs that were in the hospital. He didn't know new procedures. Now, on that particular ward, Dr. Pugh always gave certain amounts of fluids postoperatively. It was a standing order, and sometimes you could get the solution made up at the pharmacy. Other times you had to add some glucose to it, depending on how much he wanted, don't you see.

So I showed Haas how to do that; he had not done that before. I showed him how to fix the percentage that Dr. Pugh wanted and all of those kinds of things there were particularly hospital things, but that he might sometime need to know if he ever went back to the Marines. Those were the things that we went over. On anything, in fact, that came up, he had no hesitancy coming to me and saying, "Now, what's this all about?" And we'd go over it. It was a matter of teaching all of them so that they would be in a position to understand and to come to me. I wanted them to be able to at least recognize that something was wrong and come to me about it. It worked very well.

Paul Stillwell: Well, for example, once he learned about the sulfa, he would then be able to use that in whatever situation it was necessary.

Captain Jackson: Yes, because he would see what kind of patients it was given to. And this was something that happened many times in combat areas, that the hospital corpsman was isolated--as I said, if he survived. I don't know whether you know or not, but the highest mortality rate of any group in World War II was in the Navy hospital corpsmen.

Paul Stillwell: I'm not surprised.

Captain Jackson: When the Third Marine Division went into Iwo, my brother had been a member of the Third Division.* When I got to Guam, they were staging for Iwo.† I got a look around, and every battalion commander, I think, in the Third Division, and most of them in the Sixth, had been at the Marine Corps Officers School, their orientation school at

---

* On 19 February 1945, U.S. Marines invaded the island of Iwo Jima, approximately 660 miles south of Tokyo, and captured it in a fierce campaign. The objective was to provide a forward airfield--an emergency landing site--to support the U.S. bomber offensive against Japan.
† This was following the American recapture of Guam and the other islands in the Marianas in the summer of 1944.

the Navy yard in Philadelphia, between 1936 and '39. Some of them were married to friends of mine.

Paul Stillwell: That was called The Basic School, wasn't it?

Captain Jackson: Yes, it was The Basic School. So it was a matter of they took me in on their discussions right away. It was not unusual. See, the officers' club was castle rock down at the bottom and rough-hewn tables. It was nothing fancy. But sometimes we would get together and talk, and mostly it was talk about how are you going to keep this fellow out of trouble. He's just about to the breaking point, and how are you going to keep him from doing something that will get him a court-martial? And they were seriously concerned.

A lot of these men were Naval Academy graduates, and others had come from very good schools. They had that concern for the men under them. I don't know whether people realize that or not, but I knew them well, because they were my contemporaries, don't you see, plus the fact that they were also my rank, and I had nobody else on the island except a major in the Army Nurse Corps. I got with her professionally, because I had the responsibility for coordinating Army and Navy nursing, as well as supervising Navy nursing on the island.

So they were not concerned about it, and I was also classified top secret, and of course, we didn't talk top secret things there; that was too public. But you could talk about personnel problems, get each other's advice, and so on and we did. It was an interesting kind of experience I wouldn't have missed for anything. I wouldn't have missed any part of it, even the part in Japan.

Paul Stillwell: When you were in Philadelphia, this was before the WAVE program had come on.

Captain Jackson: Well, this was '36 to '39. This was before the war, don't you see.

Paul Stillwell: Right, and the point I want to make is that there were very few women naval officers at that time. Were you treated as curiosities?

Captain Jackson: No. We were the only ones, as a matter of fact, and we had only relative rank, don't you see.

Paul Stillwell: What do you mean by relative rank?

Captain Jackson: Well, if you were a nurse you were relative to an ensign. If you were chief nurse, you were relative to a jaygee.* If you were superintendent, you were relative to a lieutenant commander.

Paul Stillwell: When were actual ranks assigned?

Captain Jackson: Temporary ranks were assigned after the WAVES came in, and the nurses said, "Look we've been around here a little longer than they have. How about us?" So they did give us rank, and it was supposed to be temporary rank, but they gave us rank and called us by the rank, and we wore the rank on our uniforms. But they didn't think that the WAVES were going to be a permanent thing, don't you see.

Paul Stillwell: They were in the reserve then.

Captain Jackson: Yes. And they fully expected that after the WAVES were gone, then we would go back to the same situation as before the war. Well, the WAVES didn't go, and we were in no mood to go back to the same situation. I'll tell you a little secret, which is in my correspondence. They would not even allow the director of the Nurse Corps to wear the eagle on her hat. She wore the Nurse Corps insignia, which was an anchor, and it just so happened that the representative from my congressional district was the attorney who had seen me through my divorce. So I took myself up to the Hill, and I said, "Harry, these

---
* Jaygee--lieutenant (junior grade).

are the situations. Do you think you can do something about it?" And I told him what it was all about.

Paul Stillwell: Now, what year would that have been when you approached him?

Captain Jackson: That was after I got back from Japan.

Paul Stillwell: Okay.

Captain Jackson: I had the two years between coming back from Japan in August of 1942 and going out to the Pacific again in December of '44.

So what he did, he got somebody else to go along with him and before BuPers or anybody knew about it, before the doctors knew about it, heaven help them. I got a call from Harry's office, and I went down, and he gave me a copy of the bill which had been passed. So I stopped at the uniform shop and bought the insignia for Captain Dauser on my way back.*

By that time--see, when I came back, I had been at 1320 G Street in recruiting for a year. Then Captain Dauser took me down to her office as the assistant personnel officer the second year, so that she could look over the situation and know whether I was stable enough to go out for the job she had in mind. So she knew me, and I felt that she was a very, very fine woman. I was proud to be a part of her staff.

So, anyway, I bought the insignia, and I took it down and went to her door. The door was open. She nearly always left it open unless she was in conference with somebody. She recognized me, and I walked in and laid a copy of the bill down and the insignia. I said, "Okay, you're the first one in the Nurse Corps who will have this." [Laughter] I had bought one for myself, but I didn't put it on.

---

* Sue S. Dauser, who entered the Navy as a nurse in 1917, served as Superintendent of the Nurse Corps from 1938 to 1946. She received the permanent relative rank of lieutenant commander in July 1942 and captain in December 1942. She was the first woman to wear the four gold stripes of a captain in the U.S. Navy. In February 1944 her relative rank was changed to actual.

Paul Stillwell: During that prewar period, when you had relative rank, did you wear rank insignia?

Captain Jackson: No. We wore one stripe on our caps and then the insignia on the collars, but that was all. nothing--

Paul Stillwell: You wore, say, a gold bar if you were relatively an ensign.

Captain Jackson: A stripe across our nurse's cap; it was gold with black velvet on each side.

Paul Stillwell: I see.

Captain Jackson: And I know when I was teaching at the University of Colorado at commencement time, the dean asked all of us to come in hospital uniform. Well, I had one of my Navy uniforms, but I didn't have any from my school of nursing. Of course, my school of nursing was one of those with the fluted top. It was an adaptation of the school of nursing in the Blackley School of Nursing at the Philadelphia General Hospital. As I told you, our first director had been from there, and they had designed the cap on that, but not completely like it.

I didn't have that. That was a devil to keep up, because you had to send that all the way back to Philadelphia to get it washed and fixed, all the fluting. It had the fluting, the ruffles, the flute of ruffles. So I remember when I walked down the aisle with my cap with four stripes on it, somebody said, "Wow, well, what is she?" [Laughter] That was all I had; I was wearing a captain's uniform. Of course, there were no captains in the hospitals at that time, because there was only one captain when I was assigned, and that was the director of the corps.

Well, in some of the things that came up as time moved on, we were able to get a little better rank proportion. When the selection list came up, they gave us running mates, and the running mates were very well down the line. But the running mate for a one Nurse

Corps captain came up, and it meant that we could have one captain selected. See, the director was a captain by virtue of being director of the Nurse Corps. And, of course, if you had that rank for a length of time, it was your permanent rank. If you only had it for a little while and then were ill and had to be relieved or something of that sort, you would revert to whatever rank you were.

I had just made commander. I was 16th down the seniority line when I was nominated for director. By the time that came up, I had already had it long enough for a permanent rank anyway. So this is strictly illegal, I'm sure. I got in touch with Winnie Gibson, one of the former directors on the selection committee.* She was the one who had preceded me. I said, "Winnie, there's just one thing I want you to know. Now, how you vote, what you do is your own decision, but I have had enough time my rank to have the rank permanently. If some of the doctors are going to say we should nominate the director, because she is a director, you've still only got one captain. But if you pick up somebody else, we've got, for heaven's sake, two captains in the Nurse Corps."

Well, anyway that's the way the record came out. Ruth Houghton was nominated and one of the members on that board came to me apologizing.† He said, "It should have been you," he said. "She had to do a lot of talking."

I said, "Well, Doctor, I've already got it permanently." He had been our dermatologist at Oakland when I was out there, and he was a very nice person. He was very upset, because he had liked me when I was at Oakland, and he thought I should have had it. And I said, "No, this is just a step." I never knew from the rest of them on that board, whether they were trying to keep the nurses from getting a second captain or what.

You see, we were a threat, somehow or another, to the Medical Corps, and there was no reason why we should have been. After all, we were doing nursing; we weren't doing medicine. We weren't going to take any of their opportunities for a promotion or anything of the kind.

---

* Captain Winnie Gibson, NC, USN, was director of the Nurse Corps from 1950 to 1954.
† Captain Ruth A. Houghton, NC, USN, was later director of the Nurse Corps from 1958 to 1962.

Paul Stillwell: What was the name of this representative that put through the bill on the uniform?

Captain Jackson: Oh, I better not. I don't want that listed. But see, nobody knows that. I don't want that to go into the history.

Paul Stillwell: Well, what's the harm in it?

Captain Jackson: Well, ordinarily you don't pull political clout.

Paul Stillwell: Well, it's well over and done now, and I think it can be told.

Captain Jackson: It's well over and done now, yes, that's right. Well, it was Harry Jeffrey from Dayton.* He was a very well-thought-of attorney, and he was our representative for quite a while. His son still practices law there and so on. Of course, I doubt if his son will ever get to your archives. I don't think he had any Navy background, is what I'm saying. But that's the way.

I mean, you just have to look at a situation--now, this was completely unfair to her. She was a fine woman and a very able woman, and whoever was in that Nurse Corps had been wherever they were needed. Any of those people who were in a forward area, there would be a hospital ship somewhere there, and the nurses were on the hospital ship, believe me. It was just a very petty kind of approach to take to keep the nurses--we were so underranked, the WAVES had more opportunity for promotion than we had. I made up my mind that was going to be one of my projects as far as it was concerned.

Of course, every director tried to work on that, and I sat in on a number of subcommittee meetings, even when I was there as education director. You see, I spent three years under Captain Dewitt sorting out the education program and getting it going.†

---

* Harry P. Jeffrey, a Republican, served in the House of Representatives from 1943 to 1945 on behalf of Ohio's Third Congressional District.

† Captain Nellie Jane Dewitt, NC, USN, was director of the Nurse Corps from 1946 to 1950.

Paul Stillwell: Were you addressed by rank during this prewar period?

Captain Jackson: No. It was by title: Miss, Mrs., whatever it was.

Paul Stillwell: What were the predominant kinds of things that you would be dealing with the active duty population during that prewar period at Philadelphia? You said you had mainly those individuals as your patients. What were the kinds of complaints and problems they had?

Captain Jackson: Well, now, as an example, I'll tell you, they had to make an injury on a motorcycle a misconduct. Because the kids would come in from being at sea for a while, they'd rent a motorcycle, they'd go down the street, and we had some awful accidents that way. So we dealt with mainly accidents, or, of course, there could be a ruptured appendix or something of that kind, or anything of the kind. But it was mainly orthopedic and surgical, not as much medical as far as active duty people were concerned. It was usually the result of accidents or something of that kind.

Paul Stillwell: Probably shipboard accidents too.

Captain Jackson: Yes, there would be, because as soon as they came ashore, they'd be in the hospital. Now, many of the bigger ships had hospital corpsmen. This is why I used to say to the hospital corpsmen, "You're going to be in a situation someday when I'm not going to be at your shoulder to tell you want to do, so learn it now." Because when they went aboard ship, they would have to do the nursing care of maybe a ruptured appendix or anything of the kind, and you could get a mighty sick patient out of a ruptured appendix. So you were busy all the time, and you had a challenge. And then, of course, when you got into the Veterans Administration patients, you got into some bad orthopedic and surgical situations there too. But it was a stimulating kind of professional experience.

Leona M. Jackson #1 - 43

Paul Stillwell: You said you had the venereal disease ward. What treatment was used in that era?

Captain Jackson: Well, before sulfa, it was ordinarily an irrigation process. They would irrigate the bladder and urethra and so on and clear as much as possible, because that's where you could get serious infection. And, of course, with the women, it would be vaginal. There were certain chemical solutions that you used; it was not just water. They were chemical douches, and that was really about the most you had to work with. Then, of course, when sulfa came along, why, you could use that without the other irrigation. The problem with your irrigation is that you used it sterilely, but you already had an infected situation, and you didn't know whether you were going to be disturbing some other bacteria in there or not, because there are many complications that go along with that. You hoped you had gotten them early enough to clean up some of them.

Of course, the men themselves could do their irrigation, but they had to have some supervision and make sure that they did it. That was part of the thing, and that was why a first class pharmacist's mate, who was next to a chief, would be the person to put up there, if you had one, who had recent hospital experience. And, of course, Haas had recent experience on the sickest hospital ward, and he was well equipped to do it.

Paul Stillwell: Well, you were probably getting the more serious VD cases, weren't you? Couldn't they treat some on board ship?

Captain Jackson: Yes, they would, right away. But you had people assigned to shore activities, too, you know. And, as I say, any treatment up there was within the capacity of a well-trained hospital corpsman.

Now, when you had to do a kidney operation, you were dealing with something else. I'm not talking about in relation to venereal, so the venereal was not on the GU wards.* Now, in Brooklyn, the GU ward was a different ward from the general surgery ward, but it was amazing how many times a kidney surgery would appear in one of my quiet

---

* GU--genito-urinary.

rooms. The doctor down that way would finagle so that they came on my ward for three days, and then he would trust them to his corpsman, if I said it was all right. I mean, it was this kind of working relationship, don't you see?

Paul Stillwell: Yes.

Captain Jackson: You knew each other, and he knew that I never quibble about it, and you met each other on various stations from one place to another.

The operating room in Brooklyn was on the same floor and just outside my surgical wards. My surgical ward was across the hall, one of them, from the operating room, and then there was another one. Well, now, on this one, you kept any patients that were ill, and particularly the clean operating. We didn't get them up there as much, because we didn't have the Veterans Administration in that number. They had a Veterans Administration Hospital, I think, out on Long Island or somewhere in that area, and so most of them went over there. We didn't have the veterans as patients.

But if you got a pilonidal cyst or a hemorrhoidectomy or something, you put them on the other ward, because that is not necessarily a clean operation. You put them on the second ward, so that they were not close to the others. And then on the main ward, where the nurse's desk was, there were a set of cubicles along there with curtains. If you had a patient that could be disturbed by the movement around the ward, you put the patient in that room. And then, of course, we were doing a lot of spinal anesthesia, and those patients--now, their feet had to be blocked up when they came from the operating room, and they had to have their blood pressure checked every half hour for four hours.

So when they came back, I used to make rounds with my hospital corpsman. And especially if he was a new one, I'd make rounds with him often enough and check his knowledge. I'd show him how to do it and when he did it, I would check it until I was sure that he could take an accurate blood pressure. You took blood pressure, pulse, and respiration every half hour for four hours, and then you took it every hour for a while.

I know there was an operating room supervisor and in addition to the patients, if the head nurse on the wards had a younger nurse in training, or another nurse there, anybody who came new on the station, they would send up to work for a few days with a nurse who had been there long enough to know their way around. If you had two nurses on that ward, then one of them would take the operating room.

So it just happened one day that I had myself and another nurse, and they had an emergency. Ordinarily your operating room procedure was in the morning, but we had an emergency come up in the afternoon, and the operating supervisor was having a half day off. That's all she got one week, and she was having her half day that particular day. So I thought, "Well, this will be a good time to leave this girl on her own and let her get her feet down and feel that she's able to handle it."

So I walked into the operating room and, lo and behold, here were three of the surgeons that I had known in Philadelphia. I knew they were going to change the chief of surgery, and it was Dr. Ryan.[*] He had been assistant chief in Philadelphia when I was there. And then there were two of the men who had been residents. They had a situation where the men who were working for certification in any of the specialties would be assigned to Philadelphia, and they carried so many hours of class in the medical school at the University of Pennsylvania. That's where they got their theory, their basic theory, additional anatomy, and that kind of thing. Then their practice work was done under the chief of surgery at the hospital.

Well, there were two. One of them was Dr. Leamer, I remember, and I can't remember who the other one was, but they were all three men that I had worked with in Philadelphia.[†] When I walked into the operating room, I was so surprised. I hadn't seen Dr. Leamer and the other one. I knew Dr. Ryan was there, and Dr. Ryan said, "It's mighty good to see you here."

I laughed and said, "Now, Dr. Ryan, maybe I've fallen from grace."

Dr. Leamer said, "Well, you wouldn't have fallen very far." [Laughter] I mean, this was the kind of working relationship you had. You had no hesitancy in working, and you had no hesitancy in calling a doctor on anything of the kind. You knew that they knew who

---

[*] Commander Frank W. Ryan, MC, USN.
[†] Lieutenant Robert R. Leamer, MC, USN.

they could trust, and you knew who you could trust. You worked it out that way, and it worked beautifully.

Paul Stillwell: Now, in that prewar period you said the dependents were not treated at the naval hospitals.

Captain Jackson: We didn't have any facilities for dependents at that time. Now, Brooklyn did have some, but they used civilian nurses. We didn't have enough Navy nurses for that, because that would have been bedside nursing, not one nurse to 100 patients. And they did employ the civilian nurses for that. I know one night in Brooklyn, I got called over. Let's see, it was the night supervisor's night off, I think. They were having a delivery, and the night supervisor always supervised a delivery. There would be a civilian nurse who would be the scrub nurse, but the night supervisor always supervised it.

So I got the call, and I took a look at my wards and they were all right. And I can't remember if I was on surgery or when I was on SOQ that I got that call.[*] Anyway, I made my way over to that, and I thought, "Good heavens, the last time I saw a baby born I delivered it, by accident." [Laughter]

Paul Stillwell: When was that?

Captain Jackson: At Miami Valley when I was a student nurse. There we had two maternity units; one was Maternity One and one was Maternity Two, upstairs. They each had private rooms; they had labor rooms and the main delivery room. There was an elevator right there, so you could take your patients back and forth to the delivery room. The delivery room was on the first floor.

I got assigned to the night delivery room. Well, the night delivery room nurse was responsible for all the patients in labor, in addition to the delivery. I was second-year student, I think, at that time, when I had my OB training.[†] And I had, at that time, both

---

[*] SOQ--sick officers' quarters.
[†] OB--obstetrical.

labor rooms full. I had a couple of women going into labor in their rooms. One of the patients came to the place where she had to be taken to the delivery room and so we could put another patient, who was in the one--let's see. Maternity One had a ward for patients who couldn't pay all of their way, but they were cubicles. I mean, it was a nice ward; they weren't being given second-class service or anything like that.

Anyway, we put another patient into the labor room, and I scrubbed for the delivery room, and the night supervisor was there. When we finished the delivery, the delivery room nurse would take the infant and put the dressing on the cord, don't you see. And then you turn it over to the floor nurse.

So, anyway, I got the umbilical cord, because I was sterile, you see, still had sterile gloves. I figured if you just delivered the baby from his mother's womb, those gloves are not going to hurt to use putting the dressing on the umbilical cord. So I handed it to the floor nurse. She had been watching the other patients in labor while I was--and the supervisor was being the circulating nurse in the delivery room. It was such a madhouse of babies being born at the same time then.

So I said, "I had better get over there and see," because the person in the labor room was a colored woman. This was about her ninth baby, and when you get up to the ninth they come pretty fast. The others had made a path for them, and so I got over there. As soon as I got out of the labor room, I heard somebody making a noise. I ran for the labor room. I took one look, and I could see the baby's hair. I grabbed a sterile towel, and I just stood there and screamed, because the other patient was delivered. She was in safe hands, and all it took then was one nurse, don't you see.

Well, the chief resident came tearing around, and the supervisor came tearing around, and I said, "Look, we're going to have a precipitation here if I don't get some help." So the resident put his hand on the dressing, on the outside of the dressing that I had. I changed gown and gloves so I'd be completely sterile again. We also had put sterile draping on the woman; the supervisor and I got that on. Then he took his hand away, and I put my hands down and I got a little black fuzzy head. So I delivered the baby very simply.

I said, "Heaven help me. I've got all of my requirements for state boards, and now I've got a precipitate."

Leona M. Jackson #1 - 48

"No," he said, "you didn't have a precipitate; I was here." You were not supposed to have precipitates, and I never did have, but that I couldn't help. Everybody was having a baby that night.

Paul Stillwell: Well, in a situation such as Philadelphia, where there were not the facilities, were Navy wives on their own? Did they go to civilian hospitals?

Captain Jackson: They went to civilian hospitals, yes.

Paul Stillwell: Were they reimbursed by the Navy?

Captain Jackson: I don't know how much. There was some of it, I think, that they were, but I don't know what the situation was.

Paul Stillwell: Well, it's getting back to that now with the CHAMPUS program.*

Captain Jackson: Yes, well, actually, I was glad when we began to take care of family, because their pay was so little, particularly the enlisted men. Their pay was so little, they had nothing to go on.

Paul Stillwell: Well, few could afford to be married even.

Captain Jackson: That's right. And if they had even one child or something. And I thought, well, "Heavens, they are going out there, they are risking their lives just like anybody else, so why not take care of the whole group here?" Certainly that's the least we can do if a woman's husband and children's father, it may be one of the sacrifices, and, heaven knows, with the assaults on some of those, there were plenty of sacrifices. If they are going to do that, why not give them the break? I mean, why not make them?

---

* CHAMPUS--Civilian Health and Medical Program of the Uniformed Services, a program of paying for medical treatment provided to civilian dependents by non-military facilities.

I never battled that business of having women patients. Yes, they do take more care because of the nature of their illnesses. And, of course, young babies take a great deal of care, and small children take a great deal of care, but they've got a father someplace along who is defending the country. I was brought up with a little different set of values than some people. In my family, you were taught that we had great opportunities here, and we had obligations to sustain them.

Paul Stillwell: Now, you spoke about sick officers quarters. Were officers segregated from enlisted men in their treatment?

Captain Jackson: Oh, yes, because those were the same places where you've got congressmen and so forth. But that, of course, has been common in all military organizations. There is a differentiation in terms, but, by the same token, we tried to upgrade the kind of care that was given to--I mean, there was no difference in the care; the facilities were different.

Paul Stillwell: In what way were the officers' facilities different?

Captain Jackson: They might have double rooms or private rooms.

Paul Stillwell: Oh, I see.

Captain Jackson: That was the difference.

Paul Stillwell: As opposed to an open ward.

Captain Jackson: As opposed to an open ward, that's right. But as I say, that kind of thing, I think all of us, whoever did it--I mean, whoever had both--every place I landed, I had a bout of sick officers' quarters from time to time, mainly because I was more experienced. But, again, as I said, I like people. I did not find difficulty in relating to them and having them to relate to me. And it was easier to work in that situation, because then if patients would really need something or something bothered them, they'd let you help them if you could.

Paul Stillwell: Of course, it was in their best interests.

Captain Jackson: Well, even so, you'll find sometimes women, even if it is in their best interests, are reluctant to talk about things.

Paul Stillwell: I see. Did you find a different sort of case load for officer patients compared with enlisted? Did they get hospitalized for different sorts of things?

Captain Jackson: No, not really, not really.

Paul Stillwell: Well, they'd be less likely to go out and bang themselves up in a motorcycle accident.

Captain Jackson: No, not with that, no, not with that. At the beginning, a number of our patients were retired officers who were coming into the period of when their physical condition was going down, with the aging process. This is one of the things that concerns me. I brought it up day before yesterday when we met with the congressman who has to do with the veterans affairs. They're talking about closing up some of the veterans' hospitals, you know. Well, I am sure that there are people who are getting things that they're not entitled to, but I'm also sure that there are a lot of people who need that help because as they get older, it depends.

If you've got an enlisted man who is a veteran, it depends on what his technological background is, what kind of a job he can hold, but ultimately he's going to get to the place where he has the same situation in relation to the debilitating effects of aging as anybody else, but he isn't going to have as much resource or reserve to meet it as someone in a higher pay level.

And we have had, in Dayton, the veterans' hospital. I said to him, "Now, I am not tracking for the hospital in Dayton, but we had a home there. It started out as a home, and then the hospital was added to it. But I was just wondering what was going on with that because Reagan is determined to cut some of this out, and if he really came down and knew and looked at people, he might change his tactics a little."[*]

I don't know. If he had seen things such as people like myself, who have dealt with it for years--now, I recognize that there are people who go on relief and stay on relief. But not all of them who go on relief go because they want to go.

Paul Stillwell: Right.

Captain Jackson: And not all of them--well, as a matter of fact, many of the people who go to VA, go because of the quality, in that particular one, for the quality of work that's done there.[†] So there's always going to be a financial differential as to how people are taken care of. And let's face it, you or I can meet people with different kinds of backgrounds without the advantages that we've had because we've had an education, and I've had experience that will enable us to understand things, where someone else might not. But it is still the fact that they are there and they need help, and somebody has to see and separate the chaff from the grain.

If you do any kind of investigation, you would see one of the things that came up in Dayton not too long ago was that there was a lot of collaboration in the staff, social service staff, and a number of people were fired on this whole business of relief.

Paul Stillwell: In that pre-World War II period, did the Navy medical program treat alcoholism at all?

Captain Jackson: I never had an alcoholic on my wards; I don't know. I don't remember. Well, yes, I did. I remember one retired Marine, and he was very much deteriorated

---

[*] Ronald W. Reagan served as President of the United States from 20 January 1981 to 20 January 1989.
[†] VA--Veterans Administration.

physically, and he was also an alcoholic, and part of it was as a result of alcohol. I remember it because I had a young hospital corpsman. The situation on this one that came up was that he had done the chart, and I hadn't come on duty yet. I guess he had been on night duty, and his summary on this patient's chart was "good autopsy material." He was a smart aleck, not long out of hospital corps school. Now, you didn't ordinarily get that kind of youngster. You have to remember, they were 18 years old, you know, too, a lot of them. The ones coming out of corps school were pretty young.

And, of course, I had a kid brother so I knew a little bit how to handle them. Anyway, I always checked the charts in the morning, the first thing, and when I saw that, my blood pressure boiled. I said to Haas, "Did you see this?"

He said, "No." He looked at it.

Pretty soon the young hospital corpsman came tearing back. He said, "Where's So-and-so's chart?"

Haas said, "You're too late; she's already seen it."

So I simply left word that he was to report to me the next morning, and he was to wait. See, he left his written report there and went off duty, and I came on duty. I got the report from the night supervisor when I came on duty.

He said, "She's already seen it, and she wants to see you in the office tomorrow morning, wants you to wait over."

Well, when I got on duty at 8:00 the next morning, he was dressed up in dress blues and waiting in the doctor's office. I said to him, "This kind of thing I will not tolerate. I don't care what you think of this man; he belongs to somebody. He is a human being, he had a mother, he had a father. I don't know who else he had, but there are people who love him. You are in no position to judge anybody. Now, I do not want ever to have this kind of an episode happen again."

He drew a deep breath and said, "Yes, ma'am."

Well, it was some time later, and we had a patient that was a troublemaker, and I knew he was a troublemaker. He complained about corpsmen that I knew were perfectly good corpsmen because I had trained them. I had watched their work and the whole thing. He complained about Sowell, and I took a look at the situation, and I couldn't see anything to complain about. So I said to Haas, "Tell Sowell I want to see him tomorrow morning." At this particular time, I said to Sowell, "Look, now, I have checked into this. I've seen that man operate before. I don't believe this that he's saying about you, Sowell. I don't believe it. This just doesn't sound like the performance you've been giving."

So when he came out, Haas flagged him, and he said, "How's everything?"

Sowell said, "All right."

Haas said, "I think you're afraid of Ms. Jackson?"

Sowell said, "No, we understand each other." [Laughter]

But at least he knew what he hadn't done and that I'd defend him too. So I mean, this is all part of the kind of relationship you had. You knew each other. I mean, there weren't so many that you didn't know people. You probably knew everybody on a station. Of course, the only people who lived on the station in Philadelphia were the nurses in the nurses' quarters, and the commanding officer and executive officer. There weren't any others. As I remember, there were no other quarters. I think they built quarters there later on.

Paul Stillwell: So you would have been dealing with the physical ravages of alcoholism but not alcoholism per se.

Captain Jackson: That's right. No, at the end of the rope, really, pretty close to the end. The man was finally discharged. Well, his liver was affected and I can't remember what all, but I remember the liver particularly. I thought, "As bad as that is going, it won't be long until he will be gone." As you get to a certain point, there is nothing more you can do for them.

Paul Stillwell: Well, your professional evaluation was pretty close to that of the corpsman's, but it's not a thing you put on a chart that hangs on his bed.

Captain Jackson: Of course you don't. And the interesting thing was that it never occurred to me to think of him in those terms. I was really shocked to hear that, and I thought,

"Well, if there's anybody in the my station saying anything like that, they're going to learn to use some better ethics than that."

Paul Stillwell: Do you think that people who went into the hospital corps, the enlisted people, were of a higher caliber than the general run of enlisted men?

Captain Jackson: They were a very select group. Now, when the Marines went into Iwo Jima, the officers did not wear insignia. There was no differentiating in insignia because the Japanese had that. That was a volcanic island, you know, and they had that whole volcanic terrain, with caves. Those caves were covered with weapons, and they had that shelter for themselves. They could wipe the beach clean and the Marines killed and wounded, lost nearly one whole division in that first assault there. Their first aim was the hospital corpsman, the doctor, the chaplain, and the company officer. So they did not wear insignia.

Paul Stillwell: What sort of screening process was there to get these good people into the Navy?

Captain Jackson: Well, remember, we were in a Depression period.* Many of them couldn't find jobs, and they couldn't afford to go on to school, so they took this opportunity to tide them over. Now, some of them stayed on for a career; some of them didn't. And one whale of them were killed in World War II. The highest number of Congressional Medals of Honor were awarded to the hospital corps.

Paul Stillwell: Because obviously they had to go into exposed positions, because that's where the other men got shot in the first place.

---

* Following the crash of the New York Stock Exchange in late October 1929, the United States was plunged into the Great Depression, from which it did not recover until the nation geared up for World War II at the beginning of the 1940s. The Depression was marked by high unemployment and many business failures.

Captain Jackson: That's right. That's right. I belong to the VFW, and I get their publications.* And when the 40th anniversary of the end of the war in Atlantic and Pacific came out, they had some of the statistics. Some of this data was published. Incidentally, I was so annoyed by some of the drivel that came out on that 40th anniversary that all I could think of was, "Who in heaven's name has been teaching history these last 40 years?"

Paul Stillwell: What short of drivel?

Captain Jackson: All this business, we shouldn't have hit Hiroshima, we shouldn't have hit Nagasaki.† I said, "I haven't yet heard any Japanese say 'mea culpa' about the Bataan March and what happened in the Philippines and what happened in Shanghai and what happened every place else they ever went."‡

Paul Stillwell: Was this screening both psychological as well as for intelligence, to try to get people who have discretion and judgment?

Captain Jackson: Not to that extent, because they were not going to have responsibility. In other words, they'd be weeded out as they went along. The ones that had the best of this would go up the promotion list. In that way, the others, if they didn't get their promotions, would ultimately turn to something else when things settled down.

But, as I said, that whole thing was part of the reason that when I got into Columbia with a number of electives, over what most people had because of my entrance examinations.§ None of us who had been in there where we were seeing sick people and injured people all the time needed any further training in surgery and orthopedics and what have you. We knew more about it than the people who were teaching at the university. So

---

* VFW--Veterans of Foreign Wars.
† In the first combat use of atomic bombs, U.S. B-29 bombers hit Hiroshima, on the island of Honshu, on 6 August 1945 and Nagasaki, on Kyushu, on 9 August.
‡ Many Allied prisoners of war died as a result of the "Bataan Death March" on the peninsula of Bataan on the island of Luzon in the Philippines.
§ As a lieutenant commander, Jackson attended Columbia University in New York City from July 1950 to June 1952.

that meant that when we went back into school, for the most part, we had more electives than the rest of them. Where it would have been requirements for some of them, we had electives because of our test scores.

That was when I decided that I was going to try to find out what made those Japanese buzzards tick, and that's when I took the courses in anthropology and comparative religion, taught anthropology. I read all of the Japanese scriptures of the Buddhist background, the Shinto and all the rest of it. If you do, you can begin to see some of the reasons, the way they've been brought up. But Hitler wasn't any more vicious than what happened in the Japanese and, God knows, Hitler was the epitome of completely lost American civilization.

Paul Stillwell: In 1939 you left Philadelphia. How did your next assignment come about?

Captain Jackson: Well, I was due for reassignment; I'd had three years. Ordinarily three years was a term of duty, don't you see, and I had had my term of duty in Philadelphia. So then I was assigned to the Navy Hospital, Brooklyn, and of course, Brooklyn was New York to me. It gave me an opportunity to do so many things besides having the interesting professional experience, some of which I have described to you a little earlier in this. But it also opened up a whole world of other things.

Now, when Tutankhamen's tomb was discovered in Egypt, that fascinated me.* I was still at the age where when the evening papers came, I would be flat on my tummy on the floor, propped with my elbows reading the evening paper. Anything that came in the paper of that, I was the first person who got to it and I read it and I was completely deaf until I had gotten through that. Mother could call me, and I didn't hear her. It would be about the time to get ready for supper, you know, and I wouldn't hear her. I was fascinated by the whole thing.

That, of course, started an interest in archaeology and how people lived and how they came to live and what was the history of the world. You see, I'd had some of things

---

* Tutankhamen was an Egyptian King in the 14th century B.C. His tomb was discovered in 1922 in the Valley of the Kings near Luxor by George E. S. M. Herbert, Earl of Carnarvon, and Howard Carter.

from these aunts of mine, you know, who had given me some enthusiasm, particularly my mother's sister, Aunt Grace, which most children my age didn't have. They didn't have quite that kind of tutoring. So that was one of the things.

So I had heard about the Metropolitan Museum, and I simply got on the street car and I went to the Wall Street subway station and took the subway uptown to 120th Street, 116th or 120th--120th was the substation, and I'd get off there and go to the Metropolitan. See, the Metropolitan was not too very far from Columbia.

Paul Stillwell: Right.

Captain Jackson: I discovered the Egyptian section there, and I can't tell you how many afternoons I spent in that Egyptian section. I was avid. I read all of this and began to be interested in it and I thought, "Well, there's a lot more." And, of course, I went to other places in the museum, too, but that museum became a part of my education. Then there were lecture series there, and when I was off duty I attended them, because, again, this was opening up a different horizon. Then I discovered that the Museum of Natural History, and that was something else. Indians had also always interested me, so I would go there.

In my family, you were supposed to be able to sew and make your own clothes. My mother did it beautifully. She could draft a pattern, do anything that needed to be done. She kept my sister and I beautifully dressed for a minimum in comparison to what other people had. Even if it was a gingham dress, it was a beautiful dress. Of course, she made it that way. She loved to sew, and I suppose if she hadn't married my father, ultimately she might have turned out to be a very good dressmaker or something of that kind. She was a good dressmaker. But, I mean, she didn't have a shingle up or anything like that.

I enjoyed sewing too. So it suddenly dawned on me, "Well, now, I'm here in New York and I've been reading"--oh, for years I had been seeing in the backs of magazines advertisements for various kinds of schools and some were correspondence. Well, I didn't go for correspondence schools. I wanted to have face-to-face contact with teachers. So I went over to the <u>Vogue</u> offices and asked them to recommend the school that I should approach in terms of enrolling for courses in dress design. I told them what I wanted and how and that I was not thinking of it as a career field, but I did want to increase my competence in that ground.

Well, they recommended the McDowell School of Design. So I went over and talked with them, told them that I had rotation of morning and afternoon duties. If I enrolled, could I possibly come to whichever class was my off-duty time and they said, yes, I could. This was not the full course--the full course was two years--but this was called cutting, draping and fitting, which had to do with learning how to draft a pattern, the proportions to work it out, how to measure for drafting a pattern, how to make a pattern just from using muslin on a figurine or how to do it with an individual. If you were making something for that particular individual, how to use muslin and design your dress and drape it as you went, and then use the muslin as a pattern for your good fabrics.

I sat in on the classes of fabrics and color and line, so I had all these fundamentals, you see, for dress design. I still have the thing that I designed and made for my examination down there. It is a black coat made princess-style. It is Forstman's wool fabric, and you can't find Forstman's wool anymore; it's beautiful. This is Forstman's wool; this is their gabardine. That coat is underlined in lamb's wool and lined in silk crepe de chine. I can still wear it, and it's still not out of style. [Laughter]

One of the teachers said at the time, "If you weren't so well established in nursing, I think you would have a knack for this and could do in the profession."

I said, "Well, my mother started me when I was ten years old." So we laughed about that.

And then at the Metropolitan, I attended some of the lectures on--let me see, that was on jade, because jade had always fascinated me. And these lectures went through the various departments, picked up the jade artifacts and explained which was what kind of jade, how they were made, and so on. So I learned a good deal there, and this was all available. Anybody who wanted could come in on it and even if there was a fee, it was a very reasonable fee. As I said, New York was full of things to learn.

Then later on, it was after I came back from Guam, at the end of the war, I couldn't get back into George Washington University because it was too late to register at that particular time. I got back about the first of the year and the semester was already in operation. So I followed through on the McDowell thing by taking fashion illustration at Avid Art School here in Washington. When I finished that, I went to another school, and I'm trying to remember the name of that. It was here in Washington too. It was the course in millinery for people who were going into the trade, because I figured that as a naval officer you had to dress beyond your income. If I could produce this myself from good fabrics--and I knew fabrics because my mother had been working with them, and I had seen them from the time I was so big.

Livingston Academy, I took the millinery course which was the same one for people who were going into the trade. So today I could design and make a complete outfit for myself, except for shoes and stockings. And, believe me, it helped because whenever I was going to go to something very special, I'd take a couple days of vacation and make my dress, and then I didn't meet myself coming down the aisle.

Paul Stillwell: Indeed you wouldn't.

Captain Jackson: Well, you went into some of the bigger stores and very expensive dresses, they had a rack of them. And nothing infuriates me more than a rack, and I think part of it was the fact of when we were small--I'm three and a half years older than my younger sister, my mother used to dress us alike. She would dress us in different colors, but she'd make them alike. And when I was little I was continually told that I looked so much like my father's younger sister. I didn't want to look like by Aunt Dora. I loved her dearly, but I wanted to look like Leona. So I made up my mind I was never going to wear a dress like anybody else's once I got to the place where I could make it for myself. So, of course, you know, I wound up in a uniform. [Laughter]

Paul Stillwell: I was just about to comment on that irony.

Captain Jackson: But that had a meaning. That uniform had a meaning, and I didn't resent it at all. I had worn a uniform as a student nurse, again, it had a meaning. It identified me as a certain kind of person, and that didn't make a difference. It was only when I was out with a public group, you see, or with friends or something like that. And to this day, I will not buy a dress--now, I have bought some dresses because I simply haven't had the time to do the sewing, and I've got about two foot lockers full of beautiful fabrics if ever I get around to making them. Whenever I see a length of fabric that I like, I buy it. Maybe I'll need it some time.

I have some beautiful brocades that I brought back from Japan when I was director of the Nurse Corps and made an inspection trip over there with the Surgeon General because we have hospitals there, you see. Some day there's going to be an occasion when I'll make up that brocade. I don't know what it's going to be for sure.

Paul Stillwell: How did that hospital in Brooklyn compare with the one in Philadelphia in terms of size and capability?

Captain Jackson: It was a much older hospital, much older building. In fact, those buildings, I think, are part of the National Trust. I think they're still there. The nurses' quarters was a beautiful colonial and the hospital was too, beautifully designed. When they were saying they needed a bigger hospital in New York, I was afraid that they'd tear down those buildings. I thought, "Oh, dear, if you do, you will lose so much." And they didn't. They were up over from the navy yard aways, but within walking distance. But they were beautiful, very gracious and lovely, federal style architecture. They had been there a long time.

I used to know the origin then, and I've probably got it down someplace, I mean, where they were built and how they were built and what they were for. I think the nurses' quarters had early been a residence, because, you know, many of those old homes had lots of rooms in them.

Paul Stillwell: Was the hospital on the navy yard grounds itself?

Captain Jackson: No. It was separated from the navy yard by three or four blocks, but we were close enough.

Paul Stillwell: I see.

Captain Jackson: I liked it. As I said, the whole New York experience was very interesting, because I didn't waste any time on anything. I mean, I was on duty, and it was a very interesting duty, because again I was working with people I knew, people who trusted me, and people I trusted. And we were getting a lot of things done, as a matter of fact. I was as precise about being sure that my corpsmen knew how to do things and understood the drugs they were giving and so on as I had always been. That was a part of my creed. I mean, I just wouldn't have been on a ward under any other circumstances.

Paul Stillwell: Did you have essentially the same kinds of responsibilities you'd had at Philadelphia?

Captain Jackson: Yes. Of course, I had spent a fair amount of my time in Philadelphia on the sick officers' quarters. When I got to Brooklyn, here was one of the chief nurses that I had had at Philadelphia. Well, I knew I was going to wind up either on the surgical ward or the sick officers' quarters. And, of course, they really weren't very far apart; sometimes I'd supervise both of them. But I was not unhappy because I liked that work.

Now, the orthopedics was on the surgical wards too. We didn't have separate orthopedic wards, because Brooklyn was not that large a hospital, and we could handle those on the surgical ward without any trouble. So people in casts were on the surgical ward too. But it was an interesting thing and I always liked it.

Of course, I have always been amused--in Brooklyn one time I had two midshipmen from the Naval Academy just before I got my orders to Guam. They were nice youngsters, so I came in one night and I said to them, "What do you think? I've got orders."

"Where are you going?"

I said, "To Guam."

They said, "What did you do?"

I said, "Oh, nothing."

"Well, that's a lonesome place."

I said, "Okay, I'll live it through."

So the next evening I came in, and they were still awake when I made rounds and they started in teasing again. I laughed, and I said, "Well, you know, I've decided what I'm going to do in Guam."

They said, "What are you going to do?"

I said, "I'm going to write a book."

They said, "Well, are you going to write it for pleasure or for profit?"

I said, "For revenge." [Laughter]

I don't know where that got to, but anyway somehow or another it had got to a Marine officer who was a friend of mine. He wrote to me and he said, "Where do I come in? Revenge?"

I wrote back and said, "Well, I really don't know; it'll depend on your behavior." [Laughter] Somehow or another, somebody must have written to him and told him about it, because I then repeated to the girls and we laughed about my getting the assignment to Guam. And, of course, I was glad that I had all of these other things because I could take fabrics with me or I could order fabrics from China or Japan or something like that. Because there were ships that would go out there for people on leave from time to time. You couldn't have stood two or three years on a lone island like they were without getting pretty bored about the situation.

Paul Stillwell: Well, the Gold Star shuttled back and forth.*

Captain Jackson: Yes, the Gold Star used to; that's right. And then, too, sometimes if a transport was going farther out to the Philippines, you could go aboard the transport and come back. In other words, a way you could get off the island. If you had accumulated some leave, you could do that.

Paul Stillwell: Right.

---

* USS Gold Star (AG-12), a cargo-type ship, served as the station ship for Guam from 1924 to 1941. She was coaling in the Philippine Islands at the time the Japanese attacked Pearl Harbor in December 1941 and did not return to Guam.

Captain Jackson: And so, anyway, that was a joke among my friends about the book I was going to write. So I got a letter when I was in Guam the second time. Because one of the things that had to be done--it was one of the unfinished businesses I left out there--was the Navy School of Nursing. We had a school where we taught Navy students in nursing, and they responded very well. Now, they didn't have the educational background that we had, and you couldn't give them all of it, but you could make a very good practical nurses out of them, and they were very fine people, really.

So one of the things that I wanted to do was to get that school of nursing going again. And, somehow or other, I met one of the editors of the American Journal of Nursing when I came back. In fact, when I came back from Japan, I stopped at the American Journal of Nursing in New York.* I went up to them, and I said, "Now, what has happened since I've been gone? What new publications do you have or anything of the sort?" Because I wanted to know what was going on in the nursing profession. So I took the pamphlets and so on, and she and I came to a place where we corresponded. She was interested. It was a different approach than most people had. I wanted to see any of their pamphlets that were new. And I asked for a list of some of the new publications in the clinical areas so that I could read up on anything that might have been transpiring in the States while I was gone. This was after I had been in Japan, you see.

So she gave me the list. She wrote to me later and gave me a list of publications that she thought were particularly good. And you'll see on my shelves that I've got that second set of textbooks there: the ones that I had from nursing school and then the second set and I've been buying from time to time. Right now I thought, "Well, it's time for another library set. But not because I am going to do any more nursing, but simply because I want to know what's happening." So I decided a year or so ago instead of doing that, instead of getting--frankly, I've got better than 1,000 hard-covered books, and I don't have much more wall space for them.

So what I decided to do was get some nursing periodicals and see what was going on. Well, they're stacked. I haven't had the time to read them, but I will go back and read

---

* Lieutenant Jackson wrote an article about her experiences: "I Was on Guam," American Journal of Nursing, November 1942, pages 1244-1246.

some of it and see what is going on, simply to keep my finger in the pie. I still am registered, and with the way everybody is suing everybody, I would hesitate to take on any nursing at the present time. I think because I have learned to observe in a way that other people depend on technology, now, I think I probably could manage, but I'm going to check myself before I ever try it.

So that's one of the things that I've got to do is sort out some of that now. I've had two or three years of it, and I have to sort that out by years and tie them up where I can get to them when I want to. And then when I get Lilac Hill put back together, I'll do some professional reading again.

Paul Stillwell: How much was the pace of change in the nursing field in that era, around 1940? How much would you have to read to keep up with the advances?

Captain Jackson: Well, as far as I was concerned, not a whole lot was being published, because those were war years, and some of the best people were in the military services. I mean, the people who would be doing the writing were in the military services at that time.

Paul Stillwell: Well, let's say 1940, before the war started.

Captain Jackson: There had come, at that time, the pressure for more basic programs on a collegiate level. And then, of course, after the end of the war, there was the pressure for nurses who had the diploma to work toward a baccalaureate. And a number of the colleges would give you so much credit. You took an entrance examination, and they, whatever your test scores were, they would give you a certain amount of credits towards your baccalaureate on your diploma.

Now, when I took my entrance exams for Columbia, despite the fact that for three years I had been the education director and had been dealing directly with Columbia, I still took those. And the interesting thing was that my test results were almost the same thing as my state board examination in Ohio when I had graduated in 1930. And everything except obstetrical nursing was 90 or above, which meant the upper 10 percentile, and my obstetrical was 85. And, of course, I had worked obstetrics, but that was not my major field of practice. My major field was surgical and orthopedic nursing, but my medical nursing was practically the same grade. When you see the two together, my state board examinations, and I don't have the score on my entrance exam, but I saw them, and they are practically the same.

But you see, I had kept my hand in nursing, and I had read. Whenever a new drug came on my ward, if they didn't send it from the pharmacy, I sent somebody right down to the pharmacy to pick up the pamphlet that came with that drug. And it came to be known I was not long on a station before everybody knew that if they sent a new drug up to me they'd better send the pamphlet.

So we worked it that way, and that was another way I could keep up knowing the drugs. And I never would give a drug unless I knew exactly what it was all about. I taught my corpsmen that way, that you don't do that. You are dealing with human lives. So this helped, too, to keep up. And, of course, you had a wide spectrum of people in the Navy, and you could have a wide spectrum of illnesses.

Paul Stillwell: You cited a number of interesting examples from your practice in Philadelphia. Do you have comparable specific cases from the New York period?

Captain Jackson: Yes, I have. We had a Veterans Administration patient, either that or a retired person, I don't remember which, who was extremely ill, a cardiac patient. And in order to have a quiet room--he was an officer, but they put him up in the sick officers' quarters where we had private rooms, and I was in charge of it at the time. And the chief of medicine came along. He was keeping an eye on this patient, and he said, "You know, that man ought to have an enema, but I'm afraid to have a corpsman give it to him, because the wrong movement, and he can be out."

I said, "Well, I'll give it to him, doctor."

He said, "You will?"

I said, "Yes, and I'll teach a corpsman how to do it while I'm at it."

And he said, "All right."

So I took a corpsman in with me, and I gave the man the enema and showed him how to handle a very sick patient like that, how to insert the catheter or the hose to give him the enema, how much to give, how to let it draw, come out by itself. In other words, it was a flush, don't you see. I used the enema can and flushed until the man was relieved of the thing that was giving him gas. And, of course, the fact that he was uncomfortable with this intestinal situation made him more restless, which was more dangerous in his very critical condition.

When the chief of medicine came back, he saw the man was settled down because we had relieved all of that gas and everything. He didn't have any distention anymore, so he would settle down and be quiet. The chief of medicine said to me, "How much better he is."

I said, "Well, this is part of what I am here for." And that doctor's wife had been a nurse, but that doctor was one of my friends. For a long, long time I heard from him. And there were a couple of the doctors who had been close friends of mine under these kinds of circumstances, you see, who were killed in action. One of those doctors went down to Panama. He was assigned down there later on, and one of the doctors from Philadelphia that I had worked with, a nose and throat man, who used to manage to get his mastoids or any serious surgery of that kind onto my ward for a few days instead of the nose and throat ward--they were both down there and later on one or the other of them was killed in action, and I don't remember which one.

But I used to hear from both of them. I had worked closely with them, and it would be just a letter letting me know how they were. I'd write back and tell him what it was about and then, of course, when I went out to Guam the second time, I had to break off communications because nobody knew where I was going. Everybody suspected when I went out, because there were quite a few people who knew I had threatened to come back.

The interesting thing about the situation when I got back, as I told you, the nurses accepted me nonchalantly. I had said I would be back, and I was back, and that was the way it was. They had fully expected me to be back. [Laughter] The experience of meeting with them again and seeing the situation, I don't know whether you want to get into any of that this afternoon or not. How much more time do you have?

Paul Stillwell: Well, we'll see how far we get. You've talked about these things in clinical terms. What part did your own emotions play? You saw people who were seriously ill, in some cases died.

Captain Jackson: People have said that to me, "How do you take it?" For instance, those 3,000 casualties there were coming in from Iwo Jima.

I said, "I don't waste time saying 'Isn't it too bad?' I look at it and say, 'Here it is. Now, what do we do first?'" You see you put it on a practical basis. You're thinking, "What am I going to do to save that person? What can I do to help them? What do we do first?" This is the approach you have to take. It protects you, and it protects the patient, believe me, because if you start getting maudlin about anything, you can lose your judgment.

Paul Stillwell: Well, that's an emergency situation. What about the routine day-to-day situation on a ward, if you see somebody steadily deteriorating?

Captain Jackson: Well, it's the same situation that I told you about of the cardiac patient that I saw one night and felt that he was coming near the end. I called the doctor right away, and, as I told you, he made as complete an examination as he could do to the patient's benefit, and we found nothing there. But at least I felt that we had done everything humanly possible. I was sorry to see the man go, but I did not feel that he had been neglected in any way. I thought beyond this there are powers beyond ours, and this is the way it is. There isn't any other way you can do it.

You see, I think you have to remember, you have to something that you live by. A long time ago, when I was a student nurse, you are introduced to science, and it is contrary to some of the things you've learned in religion. I decided a long time ago, as a student nurse, not to be bothered by that. There is a section, and I used to be able to quote it, in the Gospel according to St. John, that has to do with serving the Almighty. And the end of is, "When saw thee ye, Lord--when did I-when did you hunger and I fed you, when did you suffer and I served you," something to that effect. And Christ's answer is: "Inasmuch as ye have done it to the least of these, my children, you have done it onto me."

That has been my creed. So I feel, when I have done the best that I can, that I can face it. This is the best that could have happened. I've left nothing unturned.

Paul Stillwell: Well, it sounds as if you could almost detach the emotions from it, from what you're saying, that you viewed it in a professional, clinical perspective.

Captain Jackson: Well, you have to do that, but that doesn't mean that you don't regret losing a patient. It's a very strange feeling when you see the last breath of that person, because you have the feeling that so much is lost. Now, my aunt has been dead since 1982, the one that I was so very close to, my mother's sister. And every now and then I found myself thinking, "I'll ask Grace," and then I realize Grace isn't there, things about the family. And I think of all of this that's gone now, it's gone forever, we've lost it. And what a loss it is, but there's nothing you can do about it. There's a certain length to human life.

Paul Stillwell: Well, you mentioned this period of probation for the young nurses. Maybe if they don't have that capacity to detach, that's when they find it out.

Captain Jackson: That's right, that's right, and that's the reason why you give them a period of probation. Now, I don't know what they do now in nursing schools, because I haven't been in contact with them. But we had that period, and if you gave them probation, they could still go back to their community. It wasn't as though they had to admit that they'd been tossed out of school, that they couldn't make the grade. They could simply say, "Well, I decided on a different career pattern."

Paul Stillwell: "I wasn't suited, I found out."

Captain Jackson: That's right. But this was part of what you looked for in a nurse in my generation, this kind of capacity. And, as I said, we still started the morning with chapel.

Paul Stillwell: Now, what about the opposite situation? You have someone who really looks as if there's not much hope and somehow that person pulls through. There must be a sense of satisfaction there.

Captain Jackson: Very much so. You never let go until they've taken their last breath. You never let go.

Paul Stillwell: Have you seen cases that might be attributed to miracles, that there's no rational explanation for the recovery?

Captain Jackson: No, I haven't, not at this point, that I can think of. One of the things that bothered me more than anything else in this business of dying was when you would call a patient's family, probably a nephew who was going to inherit whatever they had, you know, and you would say, "Well, now, So-and-so's condition has deteriorated and I don't think it will be very long."

They nonchalantly say to you, "Well, let me know when it's all over." I used to be furious, but, of course, you couldn't say anything. And I thought, "God help them, I hope no one ever dies alone, you know, if I can help it."

An illustration of this happened in Guam. We had wards for the native patients there. Now, if a woman was having a baby, she was not on the main ward. She was over in what we call SOQ, because there were private rooms over there. Whether she was native or whether she was white, we put her over there.

But the other patients were in a ward. As a matter of fact, the older natives, who didn't know as much about being treated under modern medicine as the younger ones did, would be a little afraid, don't you see, to be by themselves. For instance, we had some older women and men with cataracts. We would put them in SOQ, because they were private room, and they thought our eye and ears and throat man was a miracle worker because he would operate on them, and then they would be able to see. They had never been in a hospital before, but from that time on, they thought we were all miracle workers. It made a feeling within the islands that you could go to the hospital and trust people.

But in the ward, the people who weren't so sick liked each other's company. And I remember once we had a native head nurse on that ward, and her name was Juaquina Sequensa, and she was an excellent nurse, a very nice person. Of course, most of the people out there had been under Spanish rule, and they were Catholic. There were some Protestants but not many. A sister of Juaquina's had a very bad heart condition. She had had too many babies and too close together, and when she came in to us, we knew the thing was inevitable. She was on Juaquina's ward. I made it my business every day to see her as I made rounds, and the day that she died, Juaquina was at her bedside. I stayed with Juaquina until her sister took her last breath, and then she started to prepare to be taken out of the ward. I said, "Let me help you, Juaquina," and I closed her sister's eyes.

She said, "You have been so good to her," and she was on the point of tears.

I said, "Juaquina, if she had been my sister, you would have done the same, wouldn't you?"

She said, "Yes, I would."

But I didn't leave Juaquina alone to meet that grief, because I could develop and I had developed a closeness to the native nurses, and they felt close to me. This was her reaction, the fact that I had stopped by every day to see that everything was being done. I knew Juaquina would do it anyway, but it was simply to give Juaquina reinforcement, don't you see. And going through that, as I said, I did some of the things, and I knew some of the things she would want to do as the last thing for her sister. I helped her, and together we prepared the body to be taken home and prepared for burial.

Paul Stillwell: Because you might well have had more presence of mind at that point than she.

Captain Jackson: Yes.

Paul Stillwell: Was that during your first time there or your second time?

Captain Jackson: That was the first time there, because that hospital was all gone by the time I came back the second time. That was all gone. No, that was the first time. This, I think, was part of the reason why, when I said I'd be back, I don't think anybody doubted it. It was the same thing in starting the nursing school. I set up the specifications for it and wrote it to Captain Dauser and gave her the kind of faculty I needed and so on, and then I went to the teachers' meeting. The teachers were all natives that had been sent to the University of Hawaii for some training in teaching. They were having a teachers' meeting, and I asked permission of the head of the teachers' group to come in and talk with them, because I wanted them to keep their eye open for good candidates for the nursing school.

And Father Castro was there. Father Duanus, the other native priest, had been beheaded by the Japanese in front of his church, in the presence of his congregation, so we only had Father Castro there. Father Castro had been ordained longer than Father Duanus had, and, of course, I had known him better than I did Father Duanus from my previous tour there. I described to them the program that I had set up that was going to be put into effect and the increased educational requirements and the increased content in scientific nursing that would be in this program. I said that I wanted people who had good intelligence and good capacity. And I said, "If they lack some background, we'll give it to them. In other words, if we have to tutor them in basic education, we will, but this is what I want in the way of nurses."

Father Castro said to me, "Well, now, how about a girl who has an illegitimate baby?"

I said, "Father Castro, that I will leave to you. If you give her a clean bill of health, I'll take her." I said, "I saw the situation of the Japanese here, and I know that these illegitimate babies were far beyond the control of many of the girls. This I would never hold against her. I'll leave that to you. That's your spiritual background, and I will accept it from you." Because they would be going to him for confession and so on, he would know the whole situation.

But in the process, before the meeting had started, I was suddenly met by a bear hug. It was one of the teachers who had had a baby in the hospital just before the Japs came in. She was so glad to see me, and we were glad to see each other. She was a very nice person. So we started talking and before we knew it, the meeting had begun and I thought, rather than get up and leave and cause a disturbance, it was better for me to just sit here quietly so we did. After the meeting, I said to the chairman of the group, "I'm sorry, I didn't mean to intrude on your meeting."

He looked at me and smiled, he said, "For you, it's all right." [Laughter]

So, you see, you can become very involved with people. They don't have to be white-skinned. These were nice people. I came to understand them, and they accepted me.

Paul Stillwell: How closely did you work with chaplains throughout your career?

Captain Jackson: When I came back from Guam the second time, I asked to be assigned to duty at a dispensary someplace in the Washington area so I could go back to George Washington University and pick up there, don't you see. I was assigned to the Arlington Annex, and that was part of the Navy Department Dispensary.* The chief nurse of the Navy Department Dispensary said, "Well, I don't have any job for a person like you." Because I had handled the whole Pacific situation, you know, in a certain area, and this was a clinical job.

I said, "Well, now, let's get this straight." I said, "I asked to come here because I want to go back to George Washington University, and I wanted a clinic so I would have evenings free. Don't ever, for a minute, think there will be any trouble in you and I working together, because you are the chief nurse here, and we'll run it the way you want it."

She was down at the Navy Department, the main office, and this was one of the branches. Well, I was there for a while, and then sometime later Captain Dewitt, who was the director then, called me down to her office and said she was transferring me. She was having trouble with the education operation and she was going to take me over, so that was the end of my clinical association, and I went on from there.

But I don't know, it was a good assignment, and I went on to it. Then, of course, that led onto another area that we hadn't covered at all. Where did I leave off from that, now. We were in Guam and then we came back.

---

* The Arlington Annex is a large, multi-wing building near the Pentagon and the Arlington National Cemetery. It contains the headquarters of the Marine Corps and for many years had the Bureau of Naval Personnel also.

Paul Stillwell: Well, in my version of the chronology, we've still got you back in Brooklyn during the prewar period. You're jumping ahead.

Captain Jackson: Oh, yeah, well, I know. But I was using it to illustrate, don't you see.

Paul Stillwell: Well, the thing that I was specifically interested in was your relationship with chaplains. You mentioned this one encounter.

Captain Jackson: Well, it was at the Arlington Annex that I had two chaplains come in one afternoon. I said, "Well, now, look, one of you has got to be a Padre and the other has got to be a chaplain. Which is what?" So they identified themselves. One was the Catholic one, don't you see, and one was the Protestant one. Well, the Protestant one had been through the seminary in Dayton. So when he found out where I was from, he felt I was kind of a kindred spirit. I had a very good relationship there. Now, the Padre was transferred eventually, and I had no relationship with him.

Then I met the wife of the chaplain, and they were sent to Panama from Washington. They had not had any children and they wanted children, and they got down there, and his wife got pregnant. They wrote back both happy and I wrote a letter to them, and they knew that I was joking with them, I said, "What do you mean?" I said, "We haven't got a big staff down there." And I said, "You come along with a new baby. What am I supposed to do with you?" And as soon as their twin babies were born, they sent them to me.

Now, in terms of my relationship with chaplains, I had known one of the Catholic chaplains in Philadelphia. At that particular time I was dating a Marine officer who was Catholic, and the Padre got a little concerned, because he thought Paul wanted to marry me. Well, Paul did want to, but I wasn't very sure that I wanted to get married again. Anyway, he said, "Well, could you put a baby in my arms for baptism?"

I said, "Well, if I wanted to."

He said, "Well, Paul is Catholic."

I said, "I know, but I don't want Paul that much," and that ended it.

Leona M. Jackson #1 - 74

But then there were 100 Maryknoll Missionaries on the Conte Verde that came aboard the Gripsholm, and I came to know some of them.* I had been interned in Japan when they moved us from Zentsuji down to Kobe. I had been interned with some of the Maryknoll missionaries, five of them, so I came to know them and we were good friends. In fact, two of the missionaries, two of the Catholic priests, and I were in an exercise area in the place where we were being kept, where we were being interned, when that lone man from the Doolittle group went over and dropped his bomb on Osaka.† We were out, we saw that plane and one of the priests said to me, "That doesn't look like their planes."

I said, "No, it's one of ours." Of course, we didn't know who it was because we had no information, but we saw that man go over Osaka, and then later on we found that he had dropped a bomb over there.

[Interruption for change of tape]

Captain Jackson: Well, for quite a while I was in touch with some of the Maryknoll Missionaries. They wrote to me, and I wrote to them. When I went back to Guam, I lost track of them, because my going back was top secret. You see, if people knew where I was going, then they would have known something more about what was going on out there, because I had said that I would be going back to Guam. I have, at home, the letter that my brother had written me. Have I told you about the one he wrote from the deck of the ship?

Paul Stillwell: I don't think so, no.

Captain Jackson: Well, when he was--I kept in touch. I didn't know where he was; I knew he was in the Pacific. He had been in one operation which later I found out was Bougainville. He was in the Third Division. I knew that he was out there because he

---
* These were the ships involved in 1942 in Lieutenant Jackson's repatriation from Japan to the United States.
† On 18 April 1942, Lieutenant Colonel James H. Doolittle, USA, led a raid of 16 Army Air Forces B-25 on a bombing raid over Tokyo, Yokohama, Kobe, and Nagoya, Japan. The planes were launched from the aircraft carrier Hornet (CV-8). Most of the planes crash-landed in China.

would write and I would have an FPO number on it.* I got this one in May 1944. In the letter he had written that he was on deck writing the letter; it would be the last one I'd hear from him for a while. That he was going to make a landing, that he could only say that he had a special interest, that's the way he put it, in making this landing. I knew he was going into Guam, because I had known earlier than that. I had worked on some of the material that was going to be put out in terms of the geography and so on of the place.

The chief civil engineer was in Washington, and he had called me and I had gone over his booklet. I said, "Remember, the Japs have been there for a while and can be quite different."

But my contact then broke, because I couldn't write and let anybody know where I was. Then I lost track and I've often thought, some of those of the Maryknoll missionaries were very fine and I met some of the nuns on the ship. As I said, there were 100 of them. I made friends, and I never had any difficulty in dealing with chaplains or with the clergy. After all, there was some clergy in my own family, you know. My grandfather's best friend was his first cousin, who was a minister.

Paul Stillwell: Well, you described these situations in which you would have close relatives around a deathbed scene, for example, with the combination of the nursing function and the religious thing, so you might well have had involvement with chaplains in those cases.

Captain Jackson: Yes. Well, ordinarily, we had a chaplain, and if we could possibly do it, we would notify the pastor of their church. I mean, when I was in civilian nursing, we'd notify the pastor of their church. Now, in the Navy, if it was a Catholic, we would notify the priest, the Catholic chaplain, and he would give last rites. If it was not a Catholic, I made it my business to let the Protestant chaplain know. Not everybody did, but I did because that was part of my background.

---

* FPO--fleet post office

Leona M. Jackson #1 - 76

Paul Stillwell: When you were in Brooklyn in that period before the war, did you see a conscious buildup in Navy medical capability, with the idea that there would be U.S. involvement?

Captain Jackson: Not at that particular time, I don't think so. You see, I was away from the Washington area, and Brooklyn was pretty much detached as far as that's concerned. The building up of the hospital and so on was later. Later they abandoned the Brooklyn Hospital and built out on Long Island or somewhere around there. I've forgotten where that other hospital was.

Paul Stillwell: Well, I've heard the name St. Albans.

Captain Jackson: That's right; it was. That's the one, and it was a modern hospital, but that was built during the war. So I knew it after that, but not at the time. You see, those things were happening in the time that I was in Japan and then also the two years that I was in Washington. Then I went back for the other year.

Paul Stillwell: Well, what inspired this move that was going to cause you to write your book for revenge?

Captain Jackson: That was the joke.

Paul Stillwell: I know, but how did you happen to be ordered to Guam? Why you? Why there?

Captain Jackson: Because they needed a nurse with experience, that's why. There were only five Navy nurses there. We taught and supervised the nursing school, and we supervised the hospital, supervised the operating room. In other words, we worked wherever--you know, the whole situation.

Paul Stillwell: Did you have any misgivings about going there?

Captain Jackson: I had many misgivings, but I knew we were heading for trouble out that way.

Paul Stillwell: What provision did you make for your son while you were gone?

Captain Jackson: He was in boarding school at St. James.

Paul Stillwell: When had that begun?

Captain Jackson: While I was still at the office of Naval Officer Procurement.

Paul Stillwell: Well, but I mean, before you went to Guam the first time.

Captain Jackson: Oh, before I went to Guam the first time, he was with my parents.

Paul Stillwell: Okay, and he just remained there.

Captain Jackson: No, I left him with my parents, because I could think of the kind of home I had had, and I knew he was going to be all right there.

Paul Stillwell: So he just stayed there.

Captain Jackson: He stayed with my parents. And then when I went out the second time, I had him enrolled because, as I told you, the school situation, school teachers were in the WACs and the WAVES, and the ones that were left, had 30 to 35 primary students.* With children that age, you're not going to get any response in class or anything with that many children to one person. They could go a week without any of them having to make kind of a recitation or any special notice from the teacher. And I wanted a better educational background. I'd had the advantage of a good many things that a lot of children didn't have. We were not a wealthy family, but we had a high respect for education.

---

* WACs--Women's Army Corps.

Paul Stillwell: Where was the St. James School?

Captain Jackson: Near Hagerstown, Maryland. It's still up there, isn't it?

Paul Stillwell: I don't know.

Captain Jackson: It's not under the Episcopal Church anymore, but it was one of the boys' schools operated by the Episcopal Church, and it was very well governed and very well taught.

Paul Stillwell: What do you remember about the long trip out to Guam the first time? Was there any preparation or indoctrination?

Captain Jackson: Well, the long trip out to Guam the first time, we went out at the tail end of typhoon and we sometimes had as much as a 45-degree list, but I never got seasick.

Paul Stillwell: What ship were you in?

Captain Jackson: The Chaumont.[*]

Paul Stillwell: A venerable transport.

Captain Jackson: Yes. Well, my first orders were for the Henderson, and I was to pick it up at New York and go around through the canal. Then they found that the Henderson wasn't going to make that trip, so I had to go west to Mare Island and await transport on the Chaumont.[†] Well, I did temporary duty at the hospital there, and Christmastime came up and I knew there was no point in going home. I had had vacation on the way over, you see.

---

[*] USS Chaumont (AP-5), commissioned in 1921, was a Navy transport that carried service personnel and their dependents.
[†] Mare Island Navy Yard, Vallejo, California

Paul Stillwell: Was this Christmas of 1940?

Captain Jackson: Yes. So at Mare Island I said to the chief nurse there, "You know, I was at home on my way here, and I couldn't possibly go home for Christmas. Now, if you have people who are closer to home and could get home for Christmas, please give me the Christmas duty. I'll be glad to take it.

She said, "Fine." So this is the way we worked it. I worked over Christmas, and then the Chaumont came in. I went aboard, and we went out there. We stopped at Wake to let off some workers and, of course, we stopped in Honolulu. When I got to Honolulu, the people waiting on the dock for me were the Thorpes. Remember the Army Air Corps officer and his wife that I told you had been close friends? Well, he was at Hickam Field. He was at Hickam Field when the Japs came in, but he survived.*

They were waiting on the dock with a lei, so they showed me Hawaii. I stayed with them until the ship was ready to go back, and then I went on. Then we didn't make any shore stops, but we made stops to let off provisions and people at some of the bases out there--I mean, some of the things that they were just beginning to build.

I told you I had found this letter that I had written to my uncle and aunt telling them what it was really like in Guam. I said that we were five years too late in trying to fortify anything out there. For years the Japs had prohibited the Chamorros who lived on Guam to visit their relatives in Saipan or any of the other islands which were under their mandate, and that there were no fortifications on Guam whatsoever. I told them that we would be sitting ducks if the Japs came there, and that I fully felt that they would. As soon as I knew that the fortification was going on in the Marianas, I felt that they were preparing for war. That letter I had, and I can't find it.

Paul Stillwell: Was there any special training or indoctrination for nurses going to the overseas locations?

---

* When Japanese carrier planes struck Pacific Fleet warships at Pearl Harbor on 7 December 1941, they also attacked nearby military airfields. Hickman Field, adjacent to Pearl Harbor, was an Army Air Forces base.

Leona M. Jackson #1 - 80

Captain Jackson: Not particularly. See, I had had two stations. I knew my way around in the Navy by that time, and you rarely went on your second assignment overseas like that, particularly not to a small, lonesome kind of place like Guam.

Paul Stillwell: What conditions did you encounter once you got there?

Captain Jackson: Well, it was a beautiful island that had not been too badly disturbed. We had an agricultural agent out there who attempted to help the native peoples with their qualities of farming and things like that, and they had schools. They were mainly native teachers, but some of the wives who had been teachers taught school out there. And they had a nice cathedral. We had good health care for them, because, you see, they had access to the hospital. And the nursing school needed upgrading in terms of the depth of teaching, but we also had to work with our students in their basic education.

Now, this is an illustration. One day one of the student nurses came to me and she said, "You know, Dr. McKenzie gave us a formula about how to fix a baby's bottle. This one doesn't work out right."

I said, "Well, let me see it." So I looked at it and I said, "Well, now, I don't quite understand what this is all about, but I'll talk with Dr. McKenzie, and then I'll call you, and we'll figure this out."

So I called him and I said, "Michael, what is this all about? What are you trying to teach these girls in this formula situation?" So he explained it to me, and my first reaction was--Michael was from Harvard, and they sometimes get a little more technical, you know, than a girl with a sixth-grade education could understand out in Guam. I said, "Well, fine, now, I can sort it out." I said, "This one student had come and wanted some help."

So I called her and I said, "Well, now, I found out what the problem is." I said, "How old a child were you figuring this?"

"Well, the baby's a little more than a year old."

And I said, "Well, now, here's your problem." I said, "The formula that Dr. McKenzie gave you will not be sufficient nutrition for child that is more than nine months old." I said, "You remember that down here at about five to six months you're beginning with very soft foods, like mashed potatoes or applesauce or something like that. You're beginning to give them some food, and this takes up part of the calories in your diet. You don't take them completely off the formula right away, so you still mix your formula in conformity with his instructions, but you add to that to meet the child's needs. You see, your child's needs go up this way." And then I showed her how to figure the child's needs in calories.

I said, "These other calories then you meet in soft foods: custards, applesauce, strained things, strained vegetables. Now, you don't start on those strained vegetables right away. They come after the fruits and not too much of the fruit at the same time, because then you'll get a diarrhea, because they will produce that if given too much." Then I went over with her the way you increased a baby's nutrition, a child's nutrition.

Well, the next day she came over, and she had the nicest routine set up, all she needed. I looked back on her record, and she had a sixth-grade education. She didn't have the background, you see, for some of this, but she could learn. She had the ability to learn. As soon as I went over the whole thing, she knew it and she knew it for good.

So these were the things in going through the--when I set up the requirements for the school, this was part of what I planned, that we would have to tutor some of these girls. We would have to give them some arithmetic and handle it in a different way than you would in a school of nursing in the country where girls were high school graduates. I explained this at that teachers' meeting, don't you see, that until we could get the school system, as we were doing at that point, up to the place where it provided through high school, we would--in the nursing school, if we had a girl with confidence, we could give her the supplement work she needed. We would give her the supplemental work she needed, and we could make quite a good nurse out of her.

You know, I was not on the island very long until a number of the doctors with the Marine assault forces, as I encountered them, had said to me, "Whoever trained these native nurses should be proud of it. They have done a very good job."[*]

I said, "Well, the Navy nurses trained them, so what is the story?"

They said about the third day, after they made the major assault, these girls began coming in white uniforms out from the jungles, coming to the companies and asking for the doctor and coming to the doctor and saying, "I'm one of the native nurses, can I help?"

---

[*]The Marine Corps invasion of Guam began on 21 July 1944.

He said they would invariably be gowned in starched white uniforms, and believe you, they knew how to help. He said they were wonderful.

I said, "Well, this is wonderful. We're glad it worked out. We thought they would." So, I mean, this is part of it. They had certain limitations, but they were very strong in many other ways. As we increased the educational level, they could get more out of it. You couldn't go into great scientific technology; you gave them nursing. Now, you had some of the things, like pediatrics, the doctors taught it as well as the nurses taught some of it. And you had doctors who gave lectures in various things, but they didn't have quite the capacity to get it as they would have had if they had had a high school education. But we still made some pretty good nurses.

Paul Stillwell: How sophisticated was the Guamanian medical system when you got there in 1941?

Captain Jackson: Well, this is what I'm talking about.

Paul Stillwell: No, but I mean, was there a separate one from the one that the Navy had there?

Captain Jackson: No. They could come into the clinics. Now, we also had, out in the more remote areas, a small type of station which had a hospital corpsman, a senior one, I mean, not a beginner, but probably a third or second pharmacist's mate, second grade pharmacist's mate. They would take care of certain wounds and things like that that they could handle. But if it was anything beyond what they could do, they sent the patient into the hospital, and that patient was taken care of in the hospital.

Paul Stillwell: Did the U.S. Navy provide essentially all the medical care for Guam before the war?

Captain Jackson: Yes. That was the only care that was there. No, I will take that back, because Dr. Sablaun was a native who had graduated from a medical school in Kentucky, and he came back. Now, he was working principally on the tuberculosis program, but he had his private practice too. People who could afford to pay would go to Dr. Sablaun, and the others would come into our dressing stations or come into the clinics and the hospital. We had clinics for them.

Paul Stillwell: So then the Navy really ran Guam. The governor was a naval officer.[*]

Captain Jackson: Was a naval officer, oh, yes. It was naval government, unquestionably, and it was well run too.

Paul Stillwell: What were the living conditions like for you?

Captain Jackson: We had a very nice nurses' quarters. They were tropical construction with a roof and then the veranda out here that was screened. Your rooms didn't have solid walls; they had slatted walls because it would be too hot if it was solid wall. But the slatted walls and the curtains gave you privacy and, of course, it was hot in the daytime. It would cool off at night, though. It was a joke. We'd get up in the morning and you hear the shower going and if it was hot, well, this was going to be a three-shower day. If we were going out, it might be a four-shower day. There had been times when it was a five-shower day.

You'd get up in the morning and take a shower before you went on duty. Then you came off, and one nurse covered the hospital in the afternoon. All of you were on duty; the operating room was in operation in the morning, if you had patients. And the rest of those, except for one nurse, would be on duty in the daytime and then one in the afternoon. Then at night, there was a night supervisor who was one of the more experienced Navy nurses. If she had any trouble, she'd call the nurse who had been on the afternoon. She was the on-call nurse. And, of course, we never failed to get up and help her if she needed the

---

[*] The governor of Guam and commandant of the U.S. naval station there was then Captain George J. McMillin, USN.

help, I mean, if something came up that she couldn't quite understand. It worked very smoothly, and the patients were well cared for.

Paul Stillwell: Were there any specific maladies that were indigenous to the island?

Captain Jackson: I'd say tuberculosis was one of them. But that was because for centuries and centuries the white race has worked up some immunity to tuberculosis. But the dark-skinned ones never had, you see, and they got it much more seriously. That experience that I had had in working with tuberculosis patients served me very well in Guam, because I knew what Dr. Sablaun was trying to do. He was working with the Navy in doing it, you know. I mean, it was a Navy program, but he was working, too, in it. Because he would be seeing people that we wouldn't see, people who came to him for medical attention, and that way he would get them into the treatment situation.

When I got back in 1944, the only building that was standing was the masonry building that we were building there as the tuberculosis hospital when the Japs came in. And that was the whole hospital at the beginning. Then later on, with more construction as the Seabees got through with other things, such things like airports and things of that kind, why, there was also work done on what they called the military government hospital.* But they got the faculty there, but I never let loose of it. Now, I wrote back to Captain Dauser. She said she was sending Miss Sears, and I told her, I wanted experienced teachers, and she sent me a wonderful group of teachers.

But I never let loose of the fact that I was there and I was keeping an eye on what was going on, because I was extremely fond of those people. They were good people, and I wanted them to have equal. Now, I knew we couldn't get them equal, and I explained this to the girls when they came out. I said, "Now, you can't teach them to begin with on the equal of a school of nursing, where you have high school graduates in the mainland. But you're going to find some pretty bright girls here who can learn, and you're going to have to go back maybe and solve an arithmetic problem with them, or you may have to do many things like that. But this is why you're here. Do it, and you'll be surprised at the rewards

---

* Seabees is the name universally applied to members of the Navy's mobile construction battalions (CBs).

you will get on it, at the progress that you'll make." And they were a wonderful group of girls.

Paul Stillwell: Did the Navy provide religious services for the island also, or were there native preachers?

Captain Jackson: No. They had a cathedral there. But, of course, the cathedral was bombed when we went in, because we couldn't miss it. It was right close to Apra Harbor, and of course, that was where one of the landing's was made. Government House was a beautiful old colonial house that had been there from the Spanish regime; so had the cathedral. But if you were going to get the Japs out, you had to bomb.

Now, the native people knew it. They knew where to take cover, and they were glad they knew. They considered themselves Americans, you know. They were Americans--there was no question about it--and they just knew that they wouldn't be left indefinitely. They took it in stride when we came back in. As I told you, my brother and one of my cousins were part of the assault force. Well, the cousin was injured and was sent back. But as soon as I heard from my brother after he got there--of course, he couldn't give any names or any places, because the censor would pick it up, but I knew where he was.

I wrote back right way, and I told him about Maria. Maria had looked after the nurses in the nurses' quarters for 20 years, and I told him what her hometown was. I said, "I don't know where it will be now, but find her and if she needs anything, help her, and I'll give you the money for it."

Well, it turned out Maria was more worried about helping him, since she found out he was my young brother. So, anyway, I was in contact with her long before I had orders to come out. It was pretty much the same way in terms of associating with the people. And right along, of course, the first thing, I think, the troops did was see that they had something better in the way of food. When I saw the bloated babies from starvation and the situation of that island, I hated Japs more than I had ever hated anything in my life. I never thought I could feel that way to people.

The native structure there was a house on stilts, and they had steps up to them. In other words, they weren't right down on the ground, most of them. Now, some of them in the towns were built with regular construction, but out in the boondocks that's the way they were. They were of wood and wood siding with a thatched roof, and the infestation of intestinal parasites among the natives, with the filth of the Japanese, was beyond belief.

Now, we had had most of that eradicated, don't you see. There were very few people who had intestinal parasites, because they could be treated at the hospital, and we saw to it that they were treated. And those native villages were in such bad condition from the Japanese sloppiness, using anything for a latrine, that what we did was put all them under public health quarantine. We treated them, and when they had three negative samples, we moved them. And we would move them into--the village was made into a completely new village, the same kind of construction, but a place that was not contaminated. When we got them all moved, we simply burned down those villages, because burning was the best way to handle any eggs that would be lurking around or anything like that. We said the ground should not be used for another seven years, because it would not be free of infestation of the various kinds of parasites.

Of course, the worst of them was hookworm. If you know anything about the South, it was prevalent in the South, and it comes in through the skin. Many people walked barefoot, you see, and it comes through and it gets into the bloodstream and gets into the lungs, sometimes into the heart, and it was a miserable thing to get rid of. So we didn't want anybody to pick it up again, and we just declared that. Later, after I left there, when they started building so many things, I wondered if anybody had reminded them that some of those areas should not be used. Of course, they probably dug them all so and buried everything so low--I mean, they were bulldozing things--that they would be safe, but there areas that would not have been safe, where there were native settlements, you see. We moved them into clean settlements then, once they had had three negative specimens.

Paul Stillwell: You've talked about the diet. What sorts of food did you, as Americans, eat in that period before the war? Did you eat native food?

Leona M. Jackson #1 - 87

Captain Jackson: No. The ships that came in brought fresh food and, of course, some of the natives had gardens. We were not allowed to buy anything from the natives, because they wanted them to have their own food. Now, we also allowed them to buy fresh foods, as they came in. I mean, supplies were sufficient for the people on the island, as well as the military there.

In other words, they were our people, we took care of them, and they considered themselves Americans.

Paul Stillwell: What did they have in the way of income to pay for the food?

Captain Jackson: Oh, a lot of them were employed, you see. There was a good deal of construction there.

Paul Stillwell: Employed by the U.S. Government.

Captain Jackson: Yes, with things that we were trying. Remember, we were building roads all over that island. We were building airfields, we were building other kinds of installations all over the place, because this was going to be the big main place in the center of the ocean, the Pacific, closer to the combat area than Hawaii was. That's why on one of the hills in Guam, the CinCPac headquarters was built.[*]

Paul Stillwell: No, but, I mean in the period before the war, was there--?

Captain Jackson: Oh, period before the war. Well, they still, they weren't--

Paul Stillwell: Was there a native economy?

Captain Jackson: The people grew much of their food, and, of course, they could buy things and they were employed. Some of them were employed in the navy yard and other

---

[*] In late January 1945 Fleet Admiral Chester W. Nimitz, USN, Commander in Chief Pacific Fleet and Pacific Ocean Areas, moved his headquarters from Pearl Harbor to Guam. He took with him only a relatively small staff, leaving the remainder of the staff in Hawaii.

places. We had quite a number of people who were employed by the government, and there was no thought of letting anybody go hungry. I mean, they had been looked after pretty well by the Navy, and that was why they maintained a loyalty here. Even though they hated the Japs, they still would never have embraced them, because they were much too loyal. As I said, they had been with us long enough they considered themselves Americans.

Of course, their education, their schools, were on the American system, and they had had Spanish priests for a while. And then they had the two of their own, you see, and those priests had been sent to seminaries in, I don't know whether in Spain or in our country. Then, as I said, the teachers had been sent back to Hawaii, because that was the closest university, and they had been sent back there for periods of time. I think they were sent back for a year to be taught teaching techniques and so on. It was a little bit like our school system used to be, but far better than anything they'd ever had before, because the Spanish had made no effort to educate them.

Now, of course, there were a number of families on that island that were quite white, because they were intermixed with Spanish families, and they, of course, were the entrepreneurs pretty much. And, all in all, I think they had pretty good health care and, as we could, the school system was being upgraded and the whole, you know, just those things in the development of a society, and it had come in recent years, a lot of it. But from the beginning, we had given them health care and that kind of thing. They had a far different kind of society than they had under the Spanish.

Paul Stillwell: Now, in what areas did these entrepreneurs work in. Were there native businesses?

Captain Jackson: Oh, yes.

Paul Stillwell: What sorts of things?

Captain Jackson: Well, almost anything that you would have. There were groceries and there were import. In fact, the biggest Japanese spy on the island had a store with fabrics imported from Japan and so on. And we always suspected that that person was a spy, and it turned out she was. Her husband had died as an alcoholic--well, her oldest son had died as an alcoholic. Her youngest son had been sent to school part of the time in the Philippines. After he got through the school on Guam, he was sent to the Philippines.

His mother wanted to send him to the Philippines to college or Japan. He was unwilling. He said his friends had been the sons of naval officers, and he wanted to go to the United States to school. Well, she didn't want him to, but he did. He came to Georgetown University in Washington for pre-medicine. He got a lot of questions after the outbreak of war. He came to us in the hospital and would work in the operating room as an orderly, for no pay. He just wanted to know whether he wanted to be a doctor or not, and where was the best place to go to school. So he was baptized into the Catholic Church. His name was changed from the Akiro to Edward. His father was dead; he had a real go-around with his mother about where he was going to school.

When he enrolled at Georgetown, he found some criticism among the students, you know. They felt he wasn't American and so on. By the time I came back to Washington after being in Japan, he was still in school here. He was still at Georgetown. Then I went back out to Guam, and when I came back, they had cut back, at some point, and I can't remember where it was. They had cut back the V-12 programs, you see.[*] He was able to get a V-12 scholarship, and he had the choice of going into the Army as an enlisted man, or staying on at Georgetown University at his own expense.

Well, he had nothing to go with on his own expense, but he said to me, he said, "Aunt Leona, I felt that I had gotten many advantages as an American citizen." So he went into the Army as an enlisted man, as a pharmacist. See, when the war began, he had had enough of his medical school to serve in that capacity. He said, "I felt I owed that, that I was obligated that my American citizenship."

I said, "Fine."

---

[*]V-12 was a Naval Reserve officer training program in which individuals received naval instruction at the same time they worked toward bachelor's degrees. The program, which was held at civilian colleges and universities, took about two years. See James G. Schneider, The Navy V-12 Program: Leadership for a Lifetime (Boston: Houghton Mifflin, 1987).

When the war was over, when he went back to Georgetown, he just got a miserable treatment there from the other students, when he tried to go back into medical school. So he decided he wanted to go to the University of Virginia, and he gave me as a reference. And he gave Dr. Pugh, who was a University of Virginia graduate, and who had also been in Guam and knew him, as references. I thought, "Well, now, the University of Virginia is an excellent medical school. Some of the best doctors I know are from there." So I laid it all on the line.

When I wrote back to them, I explained the situation, what had had happened, that his mother had obviously been a Japanese spy, but I felt that when Akiro came to the United States to school, he made his decision and that I personally would trust him with anything. Even though I had been a POW of the Japanese, I did not hold any antagonism to Akiro and that I felt that he had the ability and the responsibility to meet their program.* I said that I was acquainted with some of their people, and I knew the quality of doctors that they turned out and I didn't think that they'd be disappointed in him.

Later he said to me, "Aunt Leona, you got me into the University of Virginia."

I said, "Why?"

He said, "When I came in for my interview, they had your letter on the desk."

"Well," I said, "I told them the truth, Akiro." I said, "I've never held it against you. You could not help about your mother. You couldn't help what family you were born into, but you made a mature decision, and you followed it through. When you could not be a scholarship student under the V-12 program any longer, you went into the Army, and you did your share there."

Paul Stillwell: Was he a Chamorro or Japanese?

Captain Jackson: He was Japanese. His parents had had a store there, don't you see. So, I mean, it was a strange medley of relationships, let's say, all the way through.

Paul Stillwell: Did he become a physician?

---

* POW –prisoner of war.

Captain Jackson: He became a physician, and then he took postgraduate work in the health field. I haven't heard from him for quite a while, the last I heard from him he was still in the health system in Maryland, in Baltimore. He was very well trained, married an American girl, and she turned out to be kind of a spoiled brat somehow or another. I don't remember how she died, but she was separated from Akiro and I think she had died in a hotel. I think an overdose of some kind of drug. So he was left, I believe, with two daughters and a son.

I haven't heard from him for a while because frankly I didn't have the time to write. I haven't written to anybody I know anymore, because the upsurgence of my own aunts and uncles who needed a little monitoring, I didn't have much time for letter writing. And this trip, I got in contact with Lorraine Christiansen again.[*] She was one of the nurses on Guam, and we were close friends.[†] When they told me about the room arrangements, I said, "For goodness sakes, put Chris with me. We haven't visited since 1954." That was when I left California and came to the East Coast under orders.

Paul Stillwell: Well, I think that story well illustrates the closeness that you developed with these people on Guam.

Captain Jackson: Yes. Well, you see, this is the point. You can make an approach to people. Later, when I went to Columbia, I decided that I was going to use as much of my electives as I could to find out what the Japanese culture was all about. That's when I got into anthropology and comparative religion taught as anthropology and some of these other things, don't you see, so I could begin to judge. I have on my shelves the prime literature or philosophy of most of the major religions in the world: the Hindu, the Buddhist, Shinto, some of the Chinese philosophy--this was a part of that course. It was taught in the school of philosophy, you see. It was not taught as religious education. It was taught as cultural anthropology.

---

[*] The occasion was a gathering of former Navy nurses in Washington, D.C., in the autumn of 1986. It provided the opportunity for this oral history interview.
[†] The U.S. Navy nurses on Guam at the time of its capture in December 1941 were Leona Jackson, Lorraine Christiansen, Virginia Fogarty, Doris Yetter, and Marian Olds.

All of the time that they were having trouble around here with the hostages in Iran, I used to think, "For goodness' sakes, Jimmy Carter, I know you're a very able man. You would not have been one of Admiral Rickover's choices if you hadn't been, but why don't you read the Koran? You might get a clue to what is going on over there and what to expect of that man. You've got a radical there. And if you follow that to the letter, you can see exactly what he's trying to do over there and what's happening and what his attitude is."* But I never got around to writing to the White House. I had too many other things to do. [Laughter]

Paul Stillwell: He had some other things on his mind too.

Captain Jackson: Yes.

Paul Stillwell: Because of your isolated location, to what degree was the hospital in Guam able to keep up on the latest in medical science?

Captain Jackson: Well, to begin with, it was the rotation of people, of staff, you see. Now, with the nurses, if you went out, ordinarily you were on Guam a year, and then you were rotated to the Philippines. And some of them went directly to the Philippines. Well, I liked Guam, I was interested in that school. I had made a lot of friends, and I simply asked to stay the second year on Guam. So you weren't that long, plus, as I say, the fact that there were a rotation of people and you had periodicals.

Now, I subscribed to a number of things. A transport would be out about every three months. You got air mail once a week, and about every three months you got a transport out, and that would be your surface mail.

---

* James E. Carter, Jr., who had graduated from the Naval Academy in the class of 1947, served as President of the United States from 20 January 1977 to 20 January 1981. Rear Admiral Hyman G. Rickover, USN, was considered the father of the nuclear Navy. He ran the Navy's nuclear-power program for many years. When the Shah left Iran in January 1979, the Ayatollah Ruhollah Khomeini seized power and declared the nation to be an Islamic republic. On 4 November 1979 Iranian militants seized the U.S. embassy in Teheran and took the staff members there as hostages. The hostages were ultimately released on 20 January 1981, just after Carter left office.

Paul Stillwell: How sophisticated were the physical facilities?

Captain Jackson: It was a well-equipped hospital, really, very well. We had everything we needed in the way of things in the operating room and so on. If we needed anything in a hurry, we could ask for the air flight. And I don't feel that in any way we were shortchanged in terms of the things we needed to care for people.

Paul Stillwell: What do you remember about the beginning of the war?

Captain Jackson: I remember that the Japs strafed the hospital. We got the word on the radio, and our radio was being jammed, and, of course, they could, because the Japs were just up at Saipan, you know, and closer than that, really, at that point.[*] We got as much about Pearl Harbor as we could, but the reception wasn't good. And, we, of course, had no idea of the total destruction that had been hit there. And it was two days later that the Japs started to strafe. And the next day, they came ashore.[†]

Well, they were coming ashore at night too. One of the Marines had married a native woman and settled in Guam. He was on his way home, and he was shot by Japanese sharpshooters and was brought in. He was just able to get himself into the hospital, and that's the first we knew that the Japs were coming ashore. They were coming ashore that night.

The worst time of my life was the next morning when the Rising Sun went up where the Stars and Stripes usually went.

Paul Stillwell: What happened after that?

---

[*] For another memoir on this experience, see Donald T. Giles, Jr., editor, Captive of the Rising Sun: The POW Memoirs of Rear Admiral Donald T. Giles, USN (Annapolis: Naval Institute Press, 1994). Commander Giles was the executive officer of Naval Station Guam at the time of the invasion. In the book, edited by his son, he reported that Lieutenant Jackson visited his family and those of other captured naval personnel after she returned to the United States in 1942.

[†] The Japanese invasion was on 10 December 1941. For details, see Samuel Eliot Morison, The Rising Sun in the Pacific: 1931-April 1942 (Boston: Little, Brown, 1948), pages 184-186. It is Volume III of History of United States Naval Operations in World War II.

Captain Jackson: Well, the Japs started going all over the island. And it was quite a while before they would let us go out and collect the bodies of the Marines and other people who had been killed. It was quite obvious that some of them had been killed after they had been captured or surrendered. You could tell by the kind of wound they had. They would not let us get them. It was several days before we could take a truck, an open-bedded truck and go out and collect them. Then we had to bulldoze them; we had to make a mass grave. We had no other way of doing it. They would not allow anything else.

When I came back in 1944, I saw all the construction that had been done on the hospital grounds. One of the first things I asked was, "What happened to the burial of the Marines?" I said, "Why, for heaven's sakes, I hope they didn't put a building over it." Because the Marines that were killed on the assault had been buried in the cemetery there on Guam; that was the regular cemetery. But, you see, the Japanese wouldn't let us give them a funeral or do anything like that. The chaplain was out there at the time that the grave was covered, but they would not allow anything else like that.

But when I saw that cemetery with all the crosses there, which were the casualties from the assault, but, of course, when I was back the next time, they had all been moved back to the States. Those were people who could be identified.

Paul Stillwell: Well, what had happened to the mass grave?

Captain Jackson: I asked, and they said, no, it had not been built over. They knew about it. Of course, they would probably not have been able to bring any bodies back from that, it would have been too long.

Paul Stillwell: What sort of restrictions were there on your movements or activities after the Japanese arrived?

Captain Jackson: Well, we stayed within the hospital compound. We went from the nurses' quarters back to the hospital, and we manned the wards, just as we always did. We still had a few patients. We had let them go if they could be taken back to their homes and be safer, but we had some we couldn't let go. They were in casts, or they were in traction or something like that.

Paul Stillwell: Did the Japanese impose a set of regulations?

Captain Jackson: Oh, yes. You reported for muster so they could count and be sure nobody was missing. And then you counted in Japanese. They taught you the Japanese. I don't know it now, thank heavens. I forgot that as fast as I could, once I got out of Japan.

Paul Stillwell: It starts with "ichi."

Captain Jackson: Yes, I know.

Paul Stillwell: Did they impose a military government soon after their arrival then?

Captain Jackson: I don't know, because we were taken off in January. We were only there through December, and then January they moved us to Zentsuji.*

Paul Stillwell: Was there any mistreatment other than these cases you've reported of people who had apparently surrendered and then been executed?

Captain Jackson: We had no way of knowing because they left us no contact. We had no contact outside the hospital.

Paul Stillwell: But there was no mistreatment of anybody in your group.

Captain Jackson: No. I know one morning, Maria, the one I mentioned before, our maid, came in crying and she was very upset. A woman in her village had been bayonetted and left out there, the dead body. It was about three or four days afterward, and the Japs

---

* Zentsuji is a town in the northeast part of the Japanese island of Shikoku.

wouldn't let her bury her. So we said, "Look, Maria, you stay here with us at night, don't go home." So she stayed with us. We fixed a bed for her, and she stayed with us. Ordinarily she went to her own home, don't you see. So there were natives killed, too, and of course, it was a savagery that civilized people can't imagine. Yet if you read some of the samurai things, it was part of the whole thing.

The interesting thing about this, which people are not aware of, is that the Japanese had been preparing an assault against us for about 20 years. They had figured that they were going to have to tackle the United States. I have at home a book, and I'll show it to you. One of the things we did day before yesterday was meet the man who is responsible for trying to find the POWs and so on, and another one who's responsible for the veterans. But, anyway, the one whom Colonel Hill worked for with all of this. He said he was dealing with the Japanese now, had to deal with them for something or other.

I said to him, "There is a very interesting book. When I went to graduate school I took all my electives to find out what made the Japanese tick."

He said, "Well, I wish I knew. What makes them tick?"

I said, "Well, I've got several suggestions if you're interested. There is one book, and I'm not sure that it's available now, that I had as a student that was picked up in Brazil by an American and was translated from the Japanese and it was, in effect, their plans for conquest. It was published; I don't remember who the publisher was." I thought later, I think it was the University of Washington, that it was published. And I said, "Even though they didn't mention it, it was unquestionably aimed at the United States. And I couldn't feel any sorrow for any of them, for anything that happened, because I think they got what was coming to them. They were working on this for years before they hit, and they had it all laid out too."

Paul Stillwell: How much were you allowed to take with you in the way of baggage when you left Guam?

Captain Jackson: They were glad for us to take our clothes. Some of us had come out in winter, and we had winter clothes. And they didn't tell us where they were taking us. We didn't know. We asked what kind of clothes we should take. And they said, "Well, any kind."

We said, "Will we need winter clothes?"

They said, "Yes, some winter clothes."

Well, I had come out, you see, in January, so I had a winter coat and suits and things like that as well as the summer things. So the whole situation was that we could take the things that we could use and they let us take. I had a beautiful set of matched luggage that I had indulged myself in to go out to Guam. And, so help me, I managed to fill it all and take it all with me. But by the time I got it home, it was a little battered.

Paul Stillwell: Did they seem to be following humane rules of treatment in keeping with the Geneva Convention?

Captain Jackson: They were not a signatory to the Geneva Convention.

Paul Stillwell: Well, but did they seem to be following that sort of practice, though, towards you?

Captain Jackson: No. They did as far as their physical treatment, as far as we were concerned, but the food and so on. At Zentsuji we said it was weed and water soup and rice, which is what it was. Mighty thin soup at times too.

Paul Stillwell: What were the accommodations like on the ship to Japan?

Captain Jackson: Well, it was one of the lower areas. You could sleep on the floor; it was carpeted. The ship was not marked as having prisoners of war, and, you know, a lot of our people from the Philippines were killed because the Japs took them out in unmarked ships, and our submarines got them, not knowing that there were Americans aboard.

Paul Stillwell: Right.

Captain Jackson: And when the men got out, if they managed to get overboard, the Japs shot them. God, the savagery from that, I don't think it's all out of there yet. I'm not the trusting person, let's say, that many other people are, because I have seen too many kinds of people in my time.

Paul Stillwell: Did you really have any idea then what lay ahead?

Captain Jackson: No. We didn't know whether we were going to remain at Zentsuji or whether we would get out alive.

Paul Stillwell: Where is Zentsuji?

Captain Jackson: On Shikoku Island, next to the lowest one in the archipelago.

Paul Stillwell: What was the nature of the place where you were kept?

Captain Jackson: Well, it was a Japanese Army training station, and we were the first POWs they'd had there. We were in regular army barracks and so on, and they were going to put us in the same barracks with our patients. We said, "Look, we have hospital corpsmen. If they need us, they'll come and get us, and we'll help with anything that needs to be done." But we had some patients, and, as I said, those patients, at that stage, were mainly in casts or something like that. I said, "They can be taken care of by the hospital corpsmen. But the hospital corpsmen will come if they get sick." And I said, "We have doctors here. We'll take care of those people." So then they put the five of us in our own dormitory, which was simply a big room, sleep on the floor, you know, things like that.

Paul Stillwell: Did they have work for you to do once you got to Japan?

Captain Jackson: No. If they had done that, we would have seen too many things.

Paul Stillwell: Such as?

Captain Jackson: Well, I mean, such as what was going on. This was the training station. Of course, they didn't think much of the intelligence of women.

Paul Stillwell: But you were kept in isolation essentially, then.

Captain Jackson: Yes.

Paul Stillwell: How did you spend your days?

Captain Jackson: Well, it was a pretty dreary kind of thing. I spent mine mostly in mending. The men's clothes began to wear out, and I had fortunately taken thread and things with me. So whenever somebody got to the place where they needed some help, they'd just bring it over, or they'd send somebody else over it if they couldn't appear without it and I'd mend it for them. And when we were moved away from there, I said to them, "Who's going to do your mending?" I mean, we kept pretty good spirits.

Paul Stillwell: Did you have a chance to read?

Captain Jackson: There was nothing to read.

Paul Stillwell: You probably spent a lot of time talking each day with your fellow nurses.

Captain Jackson: Not really, not really.

Paul Stillwell: Why not?

Captain Jackson: There wasn't anything to say.

Paul Stillwell: You had all been through it together.

Captain Jackson: Yes, there was nothing to say. And then, of course, I was amused, because when they decided to exchange us as part of the diplomatic exchange, they moved us down to Kobe, so that we would be with some of the other people who would be exchanged. Down there they gave us some of their propaganda to read. It was written in English, and it was very interesting to me when I would read that So-and-so who was so good at this or that or the other, famous in Japan, was a Japanese citizen of Korean origin, or a Japanese citizen of Chinese origin. And that's where I met the first of the missionaries, down there, you see. There were one or two Protestant missionaries and a Jesuit from Canada and some Maryknolls that had been in that area of Japan.

As you read it, you could see that whenever Japan wanted something that they didn't have, they'd have a bush war until they captured enough people to get to bring the skills that they wanted to teach their people; then the war was over. They had done that for numerous times. And this is the same thing they're doing now. Bob and I, my son, were talking about some of this not too long ago, just a few days ago. He said, "Mother, over at Inland a Japanese was employed. We didn't pay any attention to him, and the firm didn't think anything about it. They were American-born Japanese." And he said he stayed there, I think, for something like two or three years, and then he disappeared. He apparently left his job.

He said, "Not too long ago a big Japanese delegation came over to go through the plant. Who do you think was leading that delegation?"

I said, "He was probably one of their best engineers."

He said, "Well, he had access to our laboratories and to everything. The company didn't think he was anything special or he didn't give any indication."

"Well," I said, "he was probably one of their best engineers, Bob, taking the size of the thing." And this was their way of operating. This is why I said I still wouldn't turn my back on any of them.

Paul Stillwell: Are there any particular incidents that stand out from your time in Japan?

Captain Jackson: The only one is when one of Doolittle's raiders came over to Osaka, came across Kobe to Osaka. There was a high fenced area that we could walk and get a little exercise from time to time. I was out there with two or three of the Maryknoll missionaries, and one of them said, "That doesn't look their planes."

I said, "No, it's one of ours." But we didn't know what had happened. Later we found out, and we didn't know what they were going to do about us, whether they were going to get so upset with us that we wouldn't get home. Anyway, I didn't know, none of us did. There were times of stress, but I guess I had been around enough to take it in stride.

Paul Stillwell: Other POWs have found strength in unity. Did you find ways of banding together?

Captain Jackson: No, I don't think particularly. One of the things that, while we were there, had occupied us. One of the people who came out of Guam, too, was a petty officer's wife, who had been too far pregnant to send back on the ship when we sent them back, and she had delivered her baby just a day or so before. She was one of these slow southern gals who didn't know a whip about taking care of a baby. So that baby pretty well fell to me. I got hold of fabric; I made her clothes by hand. I tried to teach her mother how to handle a baby and so on. I've often wondered how she came out. She was in pretty good shape.

Now, when we went to Zentsuji, they put her in an inn and then left her there in that inn until we were moved down. They moved her to the same place that the nurses were and where we had the other people, some of whom would be repatriated with us. So my time was spent a great deal in looking after that child, because her mother was certainly not very competent in doing it. She just never had a baby, and apparently you would think she had never seen one. Of course, having some experience from nursing and having some practical experience, I could handle it pretty well.

Paul Stillwell: Having had one of your own.

Leona M. Jackson #1 - 102

Captain Jackson: Yes, that's what I say, I knew how to handle her.

Paul Stillwell: How were the people chosen who were to be repatriated?

Captain Jackson: Well, we've often laughed and said that they swapped us so they could get five of their intelligence people, five of their spies out. You see, that had to be a one-to-one exchange. They only got back from this country to Japan as many people as they could produce to send back to America.

The strange part about it and the amusing part of it was that on the ship, not on the Asama Maru, which took us to Mozambique, but on the Gripsholm afterward--no, it was on the Asama Maru, there was one man there. Something came up one day, and I looked at him suspiciously. I said, "Just what are you?" He was a Marine officer. He had been separated from the Marine regiment that was continually assigned to China. He had been on leave away from the regiment at the time when they were taken POW. When the Japanese caught him, they thought he was a civilian, and, of course, he didn't tell them any different. Well, when I got back to Guam the second time, who do you think was the quartermaster of the Third Marine Division?

Paul Stillwell: The same gent.

Captain Jackson: Paul Chandler, a major at that point. He was a captain when I first met him aboard ship--going home as a civilian.*

Paul Stillwell: So, essentially the people they were sending back were non-combatants.

Captain Jackson: That was their idea, don't you see. They were supposed to be civilians and, as I said, they gave us no credit for any military status at all, because their nurses did not have it.

---

* Quartermaster Clerk Paul G. Chandler, USMC, a warrant officer, had been stationed with the 4th Marines in Shanghai, China.

Leona M. Jackson #1 - 103

Paul Stillwell: Which, I guess, was just as well with you.

Captain Jackson: We didn't bother to argue the case.

Paul Stillwell: What about doctors that were with you?

Captain Jackson: The doctors were kept as POWs.

Paul Stillwell: What do you remember about the trip on the Asama Maru? Were you treated better than you had been on the way to Japan?

Captain Jackson: Well, on the Asama Maru, yes. That was one of their commercial liners. That was the first time we got really decent food, though I will say that the brief stay that we had had in Kobe, they made an effort, too, to improve our diets. We were pretty wan-looking when we came from Zentsuji to Kobe.

Paul Stillwell: How long had you been in that camp at Zentsuji?

Captain Jackson: I don't have the dates down, and I don't remember just how long, and I don't remember when the Doolittle raid was.

Paul Stillwell: That was in April '42.

Captain Jackson: Well, we were at Kobe then. That's where I saw the one raider go over to Osaka, where they did drop one bomb, because that was one of the very big industrial cities in Japan. So it would have been from the time they got us there. We were aboard ship from January. It was cold and it was snowing when we got into Japan, so it was still very cold. It took us two or three weeks, something like that, I think, and then we were at Zentsuji. All we had in the way of heat at Zentsuji was a charcoal pot. You could go up and warm your hands and freeze in your shoulders, you know. But fortunately we had all brought winter clothes. We'd all come out at the time when we brought winter clothes with us, so we did have them. Now, some of the men had only summer gear.

Paul Stillwell: Did you have any contact with Japanese people other than guards or people officially in charge?

Captain Jackson: Well, we did in Kobe. There was a Japanese housekeeper and Japanese people in charge, because, we, after all, were internees, you know. So they kept an eye on us.

It was amusing, though; there are some things that are international. I have always liked cats, and I have some in my house. A cat came into one of the rooms in this particular place in Kobe and had a litter of kittens. Well, I was one of the first to discover it, and of course, I had to look after the kittens each day. I mean, I had to go and see if they were all right. I wanted to be sure the Japs weren't feeding one of them to us. You know, they do eat all kinds of meat over there. I'm not kidding. [Laughter]

So, anyway, one day when I went in they were gone. The housekeeper was a friendly nice woman, but she didn't speak English and, of course, I didn't speak Japanese, but we tried to give sign language, however, sometimes to communicate. And I took a look at her, and I said, "Meow, meow." They were gone.

And she looked at me for a minute, and then her eyes sparkled, and she smiled and she went--the cat had carried them away. [Laughter]

Paul Stillwell: The mother cat had taken them.

Captain Jackson: Yes, had taken them away. And I thought, "Well, now, in Japan and in America the cats still carry their kittens away."

Paul Stillwell: Was the Japanese ship marked to show externally that there were POWs on board?

Leona M. Jackson #1 - 105

Captain Jackson: Well, coming back, yes. They had to meet the Geneva Convention. They were very definite. They went lighted day and night, and there were red crosses on the ships. That was part of the negotiations. The Japanese had to obey the convention that time, because that was part of the Geneva Convention.

Paul Stillwell: That was the quid pro quo for getting their own people back.

Captain Jackson: Yes, that was right. And I'm sure they had no idea that one of these days I was going to be in a forward area seeing that as much damage was done to them as possible. [Laughter]

Paul Stillwell: Well, you wouldn't really be the instrument of that damage.

Captain Jackson: No, no. But when I was saving people, I was cutting down their majority, which I fully intended to do. I mean, when I was working to see that people were saved.

Paul Stillwell: Right.

Captain Jackson: I wasn't doing it all myself, but I was providing the people that did it, and it was one way to get back at them.

Paul Stillwell: Do you recall anything about the exchange process at Mozambique?*

Captain Jackson: Oh, yes. The ship docked. The Gripsholm was already there when we got in, and the Japanese were aboard. And, of course, once both ships, the Conte Verde

---

* Lourenço Marques was in what was then known as Portuguese East Africa. The Gripsholm, a Swedish passenger liner, brought approximately 1,500 Japanese and Thai nationals to exchange for American and other Allied nationals who had been interned in Japan and Japanese-occupied countries. The Gripsholm departed Lourenço Marques on 28 July 1942.

and the <u>Asama Maru</u> got in, then the people in charge on the ships got together and arranged how the exchange procedure would work out.

Paul Stillwell: Where did it take place? Was there a specified location?

Captain Jackson: There at the dock.

Paul Stillwell: Was it actually one-for-one, one person would go one way and one the other?

Captain Jackson: Well, no, that would have been settled when they put the people aboard, that there were equal numbers. But they were counted to be sure they were all there.

Paul Stillwell: Are there any other returning Americans you remember other than Paul Chandler? There was a U.S. naval officer, Henri Smith-Hutton.[*]

Captain Jackson: Oh, yes, I knew Henri Smith-Hutton and his wife.

Paul Stillwell: They had been at the embassy in Tokyo.

Captain Jackson: Yes, I knew them. He was the naval attaché. In fact, I knew all the embassy people. Chip Bohlen too.[†] When Admiral Pugh went up to Russia for some reason during the time that I was director, when he came back, he said, "I had an inquiry about you in Moscow."

I said, "You mean, Chip Bohlen?"

"Oh," he said, "the ambassador."

---

[*] Lieutenant Commander Henry H. Smith-Hutton, USN, was naval attaché, in Tokyo when the war started. The oral history of Smith-Hutton, who retired as a captain, is in the Naval Institute collection. An excerpt dealing with his period in captivity appears on pages 243-248 of Paul Stillwell's <u>Air Raid: Pearl Harbor!</u> (Annapolis: Naval Institute Press, 1981).

[†] Charles Bohlen was a career diplomat who subsequently served as an ambassador. He was later considered the leading Sovietologist in the U.S. Foreign Service.

I said, "Yes. I've known him a long time, Dr. Pugh." He had been named ambassador to Russia, and I had been named director of the Nurse Corps. Then another time I got out to Japan with Admiral Hogan when he was making a trip out there.* I suddenly got a message that there was a call from the embassy and I said, "Oh?"

They said, "Yes, there is a call on the line. They're asking for you." And they said, "It's the ambassador."

I said, "Oh, yes."

They looked at me so funny and said, "You know him?"

I said, "Oh, yes, I've known him for years." He was one of the people who had been in China, and then he had also been in Japan. He was part of the embassy staff, and he had gone back to Japan as the ambassador. So you formed relationships. This isn't pertinent here, but it may be of interest to you. Chip Bohlen died of cancer, and I have always felt that that was probably triggered by the espionage in our embassy in Russia, because he was a very, very well prepared man.† He spoke Russian, you know, fluently, and that was his third tour of duty in the embassy in Russia, when he was there as the ambassador. He was a very well prepared man.

The State Department, at that time, had some up-and-coming Foreign Service officers who were willing to learn the language of the area that they wanted to work in. They had had so many that were political appointees. And your Foreign Service officers would work his way up so far, and then he couldn't get any farther because it was politics. And yet, many of them had the language fluency.

Paul Stillwell: Understanding of the culture.

Captain Jackson: The understanding of the culture and the whole thing. Chip was a graduate of Princeton, and he had taken some of the those things there. He prepared for the diplomatic service.

---

*Rear Admiral Bartholomew W. Hogan, MC, USN, served as the Navy's Surgeon General from 1955 to 1961.
† Bohlen died 1 January 1974.

Leona M. Jackson #1 - 108

Paul Stillwell: What do you remember about the trip back on the Gripsholm?

Captain Jackson: Well, the Gripsholm, of course, we had to stop in Brazil, at the capital.*

Paul Stillwell: Rio de Janeiro.

Captain Jackson: Yes. And we came in there, of course, and there was the Curquevada and the whole thing in Brazil; it was fine. Because we had Latin American diplomats on the ship, too, that we were exchanging, and they would go from Brazil to their own countries in South and Central America. Then, when we came on up to the United States, we, of course, came into the port of New York, but we were actually anchored over at Hoboken, which is in New Jersey, right beside the New York Harbor. It's more a commercial landing than it is a passenger ship landing. But, believe me, that morning that we were coming in-- we were coming in early--you can't imagine how many were on the rail watching for the Statue of Liberty.†

Paul Stillwell: Please describe your reaction on getting back to this country.

Captain Jackson: Well, all I could think of was that, "I am home. I didn't expect I'd make it and I'm living on borrowed time." That's why I had said to you that if I wrote the book it was going to be on borrowed time and the things that were open to me in the years that I had the borrowed time and how I had made use of the borrowed time, to the benefit of the Navy, I hoped.

Paul Stillwell: Did you then get an opportunity to go visit your family?

Captain Jackson: After I had checked in, yes. I checked into the director of the Nurse Corps, who needed a report, don't you see, and we all had 30 days' leave. I began mine

---

* The Gripsholm reached Rio on 10 August 1942.
† The arrival in New York was on 25 August 1942.

after I had seen Captain Dauser. The day before we left Zentsuji, many of the men came to us and said, "If you get home before we do, will you write to our families?"

We said, "Of course, we will."

That night their farewell to us was a singsong outside our dormitory door. One the dentists, the man who had been the Navy dentist on the island, came to me and said, "Jack, if you get home before I do, will you write to my girl and ask her to wait for me?"

I said, "Sure, I will, give me your name and address." And he did. But when we were ready to leave, we couldn't take any of that with us, because the Japanese did not have enough interpreters to know what this was. They thought it could be some intelligence information. So we couldn't take them. Well, when we got back to Washington, before we went home, I said, "I'll take the hospital group." And Jo Fogarty had married one of the Foreign Service officers in Lourenço Marques. He did not have his complete Foreign Service tour of duty done at the time the Japs took over. He was in the embassy in Tokyo. And so he was being assigned to French Equatorial Africa to finish his overseas assignment.

So they went to French Equatorial Africa for assignment; they were married in the cathedral at Lourenço Marques. In fact, when I called the other evening--when Fred Hyatt asked me to call Josie, and she wasn't sure she'd be able to come up. I called her; he gave me her telephone number. She said she was going to call him the next day, but he hoped that she would come. Well, when I called her, she answered and I said, "Jo?"

She said, "Who is this?"

I said, "Well, it's been a long time. The last time I saw you was in the cathedral at Lourenço Marques."

She said, "Who in the world?"

I said, "Leona. Who else did you expect?"

She said, "For goodness' sakes."

So I talked with her and she told me--I hadn't been in touch with her for years, because they went their way in the diplomatic corps, and I went my way in the Navy. Not that we weren't friends. We still were fond of each other, but our paths just didn't cross. So then, again, this is not pertinent to my history, but it gives you a little insight into what it was about. When I talked with her, she said, well, she didn't really feel that she could make it in that time. You see, the point of it was, that nobody could seem to give them any addresses on these people. And when he called me, I said, "Well, I can tell you where you can get the addresses. I know that the man who writes the Zentsuji newsletter every quarter does have addresses on them, because he sends these things to them through the mail, and every now and then I see something mentioned about it."

So I gave him that name, and he made the telephone calls, and that's how, somehow or other, he got in touch with Jo. After I had talked with Jo a little bit, I said, "Well, how long have you been alone, Jo?." She told me she had been down there for three years. I said, "Well, the address that was given in the Zentsujian was still in Arlington."

She said, "Well, I've been down here three years."

And I said, "By the way, Jo, how long have you been alone?"

And she said, "Well, Fred died in the '60s, in '62, more than 20 years."

Then I found that she had evidently had some malignancies; she's had some surgeries. She said she had lost a good portion of her intestine with surgery, and her voice--this again, is the nurse who learned before we had all the gadgets that monitored for us. Her voice told me that she was in poor condition, that she was ill. She said she had moved down there, she wanted to be someplace where she knew there would be somebody to take care of her when she couldn't take care of herself with Fred gone.

I said, "Don't you have any family?"

She said, yes, she had a brother not too far away and she had a nephew who is her godson.

I said, "Well, just remember that if anything comes up"--and I told her that I'd had this trouble with my eyes, but I said, "I don't expect this is going to be a kind of thing that's going to completely inhibit my doing what I want to do." And I said, "If anything ever comes, I may have to have surgery. I know I'll have to have surgery with the cataracts. I may have to have another laser surgery on the right eye. But when the thing is all sorted out, if anything ever comes and you can't get somebody else, don't hesitate to call me, because I can get down to Florida pretty quickly."

But there's that kind of relationships. When I heard that they were putting two of us in a room, which was fine because it gave us a chance to visit, I said, "Well, how about getting Lorraine Christiansen and I together." I said, "You know, we were both in Guam."

They said, "Fine."

When Chris came in here she said, "Well, this is wonderful."

We hadn't seen each other since '54, but you never lose that closeness, somehow or another. You've been through a lot together, and you feel that you have a special relationship and you do. Sometimes these things are even stronger than family relationships. Not in my case, but it many cases it can be.

Paul Stillwell: What sort of homecoming did you get from your family?

Captain Jackson: Well, they were very relieved, let's say, to see me.

Paul Stillwell: Had they known of your fate?

Captain Jackson: Well, they knew, but didn't know for months that we were still alive.

Paul Stillwell: So you had not been able to communicate with them at all.

Captain Jackson: No. They didn't know that we were alive. That's why my brother waited until I got home before he joined the Marines. But he was only 18 then. He had his 21st birthday in Guam, and I happened to mention one evening to the colonel of one of the battalions down there, somehow or other I was going to get the hospital cook to make a birthday cake. I said, "My brother is having his 21st birthday."

He said, "Well, for heaven's sake, I'll have the cook make it, because," he said, "I've got a nephew who's a PFC in the Marine Corps, and I'll just ask him up, and we'll feed the boys a birthday cake."* So that's what he did. There was an Army nurse and myself and this colonel and one of the other Marine officers and the two boys. We all had some of

---
* PFC--private first class.

their birthday cake, and then we sent them back to their quarters with the cake. It was one of these big things, oh, I guess, almost half as big as this desk.

We said, "You can give it to the rest of them." My brother's name is Roy, and my sister used to call him Ripper, because he was always into something. He said, "Well, you can take it back and share it with the rest of them." So whether anybody else got any of it or whether they sat down and consumed it themselves, I've never asked him.

Paul Stillwell: You said the Japanese had confiscated this list that you were taking about people.

Captain Jackson: Oh, I forgot to put that in. When we came to Washington we went to BuPers. We asked them to give us the last roster of the people that they knew were assigned then. And then Chris and Doris took the Marine Corps, and they went to Marine Corps Headquarters and asked them if they would give them the list. Then, as soon as we got home, we started writing letters. And long before I got around the list, I began getting letters from the ones who hadn't received letters yet, don't you see. So I wrote back and said, "For heaven's sake, tell people not to bother to write. I'm going to write to all of you. I've got the list, and I'm writing as fast as I can."

Paul Stillwell: Just telling them that you had seen them okay after the invasion.

Captain Jackson: Yes, that the last time that I had seen them and this was the situation as I left them. Now, a couple of my hospital corpsmen's mothers continued to write to me. I was back in Guam, of course, when we brought the POWs from Japan through Guam. One of them was this one hospital corpsman who had been badly injured. And his mother and I had kept a correspondence through the two years that I was there until I went back again, and then, of course, I couldn't write to her.

When I saw him, the first thing he said to me was, "Thank you for writing to my mother."

I said, "Well, I told you I would."

Paul Stillwell: How did he know that she was in touch with you?

Captain Jackson: His mother had gotten a letter through to him.

Paul Stillwell: I see.

Captain Jackson: You see, he was still injured when he got back. I mean, he needed prolonged treatment, because the Japanese didn't have that kind of technique. He said that was the first thing. And I said, "Well, I told you I'd write to her," I said, "She was the first person I wrote to."

He said, "Well, she wrote to me and told me you had written to her." He said, "I want to thank you." So I'm looking forward to seeing him next year at the Zentsuji reunion here in Washington.

Paul Stillwell: That should be interesting.

Captain Jackson: Well, of course, he's a grown man in his 50s now, more than his 50s.

APPENDIX

Narrative by: Mrs. Leona Jackson, Lt.(jg)
Navy Nurse
Capture of Guam by the Japanese. Internment of occupants, nurses, etc. by Japanese. December 9, 1941.

Mrs. Jackson, a Navy nurse, was captured on Guam shortly after the start of the war. She tells a fluent story of her experiences as a Jap prisoner on Guam and later on the mainland of Japan. She describes the sidelights of the Doolittle Tokyo raid which occurred while she was a prisoner. Mrs. Jackson was repatriated on the GRIPSHOLM in June 1942.

Film No: 36 Copy No. 1 of two copies.
Recorded: March 31, 1943

OFFICE OF NAVAL RECORDS AND LIBRARY

This is Leona Jackson, Chief Nurse, United States Navy. This recording is being made March 31st 1943, Bureau of Medicine and Surgery, Washington, D. C.

For most people in this country the war began with Pearl Harbor, but I was not on Pearl Harbor. It began for me, and for four other members of our corps and the staff of doctors and hospital corpsmen and the rest of the Naval administrative staff on the island, in Guam. We had our own hands full down there. We had just had word of the bombing of Pearl Harbor when the Japanese came over to pay us a call. I might add that their calling cards were a little bit explosive. When they came over I wondered for an instant, I think, if it was the Clipper returning but there hadn't been any Clipper in the day before and as the sound came nearer, I realized that it couldn't be a Clipper, it didn't sound like a PBY which had come sometimes to the island on their way to the Far East, so, the inevitable conclusion was that it must be the Japs. They had come over the island before, photographic mission, reconnaissance, so we weren't particularly surprised at that. Just about that time the Chief Nurse knocked on my door and said that word had just come in that the Japs had bombed Pearl Harbor - They'll probably be here next. I remember thinking rather idly, well, why did she say they would be here, they were here. But my only comment was - "So, it had come at last."

I wasn't surprised at the Japanese attack, and I think for many of the people there it didn't come as a surprise. The situation had been tense and the Governor had sent the families from the island several weeks previous to the actual outbreak of war. I think our first reaction was one of relief that we didn't have the women and children there on the island. I was scheduled for afternoon duty and I knew that there wouldn't be any casualties reported into the hospital for a little while so I leisurely finished my shower and got into a uniform. The other nurses were on duty in the hospital, and I realized that somebody was going to have to relieve them in the afternoon. In about an hour, I should say, the casualties had come in. The first objectives of the Japanese raid had been the PENGUIN, which was one of the station ships there, and the Marine barracks, and the Marine post at Sumay. The report came to us that the PENGUIN had been attacked and that the Skipper had scuttled her. A little while later the Skipper himself (Lt. Hanland) was brought in and we knew then that the reports were true, we got the information straight from him. The Marines had brought in some casualties. They were the usual sort of thing which you would find in incidents like this. The radio operator had been injured, skull fracture, I believe, when the Japanese bombed communications. That seems to have been their first objective, communications. That plan of attack was used in order to keep us from getting any information of the attack off the island. I may add that they never did get the communication station. They were able to jam it with their radio which they had located on probably SIAPAN or ROTA but they never did put our communication system mechanically out of order. They rendered it ineffective.

The Japanese raided twice the first day. The first raid consisted of nine planes. I had gone on duty after lunch and was making rounds in the hospital when we heard them come over again. They came low over the hospital attempting to get the communications building, which was not awfully far from our ward. The clatter was terrific but there really wasn't anything to get excited about because there was no place to go. The island was completely and entirely unfortified and so I think most of us just went on with our routine things as they would be done in ordinary circumstances. When we left and took our turns at sleep that night I think each of us

- 1 -

wondered if the Japanese would attempt a landing, but dawn came and no Japanese on the island at least as far as we knew, and the day began again and the Japanese began again. This time there were three raids. The last raid of the day the Japanese were strafing as they came over, we never did know whether they were just trying to get the communications or whether they were just plain strafing. There weren't a lot of bullets came into the hospital, I think just two or three, something of that sort landed in the various wards as they came over. There weren't a whole lot of casualties from the second day. The roads were filled during the two days with natives who were making their way from Agana to their ranches in the interior of the island. They had been warned that in event of hostile aircraft action they should leave the settled areas and go into the cover of the palm jungles in the interior.

The actual landing on the island came about 3:30 I think we heard the first shots on the third morning of war. I was awakened from sleep by the sound of shots and walked out of my room onto the Lanai and everything looked so peaceful it seemed very difficult to realize that war had broken out in the Pacific. I listened and things were quiet, I noticed a curtain in the room next door to me move and said to Miss Fogarty - "I wonder if that is a landing party." and she said - "Well, it might be a landing party, or perhaps it is just the sentries firing at looters." So, both of us waited and in about half an hour we heard shots again. This time I said - "Joe, I am quite sure that it's a landing party, and I am going to make rounds in the hospital and see what's going on over there." and she said - "I'll go with you." So, all of us went over to the hospital. The shots came closer and increased in volume as the Japs proceeded toward Agana. We had made our rounds and had come down to the library which was just off the emergency room and which we thought would be the most logical place to get any news or information. The Captain at the hospital had sent a messenger over to the government house asking if he knew anything about a Japanese landing on the island, and the only word was that they had received no word. Evidently, they had received no word because the sentries had been killed by the Japanese as they landed. However, it was quite evident that there was something more than usual afoot. They, that is the Japanese, came into Agana about six o'clock that morning. The first actual word of their landing on the island was brought to us by Bill Hughes who was one of the Public Works foremen. He and his native wife and brother-in-law had been coming in toward Agana from their ranch and they ran into an ambush of Japanese soldiers. At first they had thought that it was a Marine patrol, because of the darkness all uniforms look much alike, but as the Japanese jumped onto the running-board of the car they realized that it was Japanese and not our own Marines, and he had thrown the car into gear and thrown the Japanese off as he accellerated it and had left them shooting at him, but before he got away from them they had bayoneted his native wife and brother-in-law. He himself had been bayoneted, but he had brought them into the hospital for treatment. Then we knew that the Japanese were on the island. The firing ceased about dawn, about six o'clock. I think the most bitter moment in my life came at sunrise when standing in the library door I saw the Rising Sun on the flag pole where the day before the Stars and Stripes had proudly flown.

The Japanese appeared in the hospital compound about 8:30, I think, a few of them had been in during the actual landing but they appeared in force about 8:30. They used the hospital as a headquarters at first, I think they probably thought that if the Americans came over to retaliate they wouldn't fire on the hospital and that that was the reason they used it, to save their own skins. The prisoners, the American officers and men who were stationed on the island, were captured or required to surrender and/as they did they were brought into the hospital compound. The officers were lodged in the upper section of SOQ and the men downstairs. Conditions were extremely crowded, of course. The only extenuating circumstances were the fact that it was

1014

tropic construction, and there was plenty of ventilation. They were retained in the hospital for several days after the Japanese occupied the island. At first things were chaotic. The Japanese definitely didn't have a grasp of the situation, their soldiers ran wild, with all of the attendant ills of the Japanese soldier when he runs wild. The prisoners were moved from the hospital after several days. The officers were put in the KCK hall which which was on the cathedral compound next door to us. The enlisted men and the civilians were put in the cathedral itself. The Churches, I think throughout the island, had been used or were being used as barracks, as were the schools. At the hospital the American nurses remained, the native nurses remained, the Commanding Officer was allowed to designate two doctors and a warrant officer as Administrative Staff. It was quite logical that he would choose the Chief of Medicine who was also the laboratory chief and the chief of surgery. He chose one warrant pharmacist, who had been in the administrative end of it, who could be responsible for the commissary and the dispensation of such food as the Japanese left to us.

The Japanese had taken over by this time all of the hospital except for one ward. Part of the hospital they used as barracks, one ward of it, I think, they used as a ward. But we had nothing to do with those patients, the Japanese did not want us to know the extent of their casualties. From time to time new ones were brought in. From time to time reports were brought to us by natives who managed somehow or other to get word in of sailors who had been brought in and were without clothes or were dripping wet and that sort of thing, so we judged the Japanese were having a little bit of difficulty in some of their landings and that they might be having difficulties quite a distance away from the island and bringing their casualties in here for treatment. The hospital ward which was left to us housed all sorts of patients. It was probably the most amazing ward I'll ever see unless I get back in some active duty. We had war casualties there, and natives, and men and women and children, we even had a Cassearian section for variety. We were able to take excellent care of these people because the Japanese had confined the native nurses to the compound too, and inasmuch as there were about 30 of them, some of them had gone to their homes before the Japanese landing and didn't return, but we still had an adequate force. Several hospital corpsmen had been retained on the compound and the operated the laundry and the galley. The rest of them had been sent over to the Church with the other prisoners.

Life went on this way, and it was extremely uncomfortable. We remained in our quarters but we had no privacy in those quarters. We never knew when or how many people would be stalking through looking things over, picking up what they wanted. About two days after the Japanese occupied the island a big Japanese Navy Captain came in, seated himself in our living room and said - "Have you had any news?" Well, of course, we wouldn't compromise any of the natives who were bringing news to us, so, we said - "No." So, he said - "So sorry to tell you, your fleet all sunk." and we said - "Well, too bad." and let it go at that. The island was full, of course, of Japanese propaganda, Japanese version of the news. However, one rumor became current and seemed to have some foundation, that we were being moved from the island. This rumor was proven true when on Christmas day we were told to inventory all of our personal possessions, pack them. To pack a bag containing only the things that we ourselves could carry. The rest of our things it seems were to be stored for us, so the Japanese said, would be sent to us later if we needed them. We asked what sort of things we should put in this bag, if we needed heavy clothes. Oh! No, we were going south, we wouldn't need any. Just the same each of us took a heavy coat. We had come out and had had the heavy coats while we were crossing.

1015

The men were very much more unfortunate than we were. None of them, I think, with the exception of one, either Dr. Moe or Capt. Todd, USMC, had been allowed to return to their quarters to get anything, and the first few days after the Japanese landing their house girls had been able to bring in something in the way of clothing to them. The Japanese had looked things over and anything that they thought might be used in the future they refused to allow the officers and men to have. A few articles of their clothing they did allow them to have, however. But most of them had only the things which they wore on their backs. One officer who finally through some oversight of the Japanese gained permission from one of the petty officialdom to get to his home found that everything of any value had been stripped from it, and the things, the articles of clothing the Japanese couldn't use they had ripped up with a bayonet so that no one else could use them. To all inquiries the Japanese said the houses were sealed, they were under the protection and jurisdiction of the Japanese military, would be held for them. They went over the island and stripped it, they took food, they took equipment, sewing machines from the natives, everything. The local Japanese had proved a very effective fifth column: Mrs. Sawada, Mrs. Dejima, Shinohara, Shimizu, to some extent though I don't know how much. One of the officers later had said to Shimizu, when it became known that the Japanese, a small force of them had landed on one of the remote points of the island about two days before the outbreak of war, and "Well, if you knew they were here, why didn't you tell me?" and Shimizu said - "Well, they were at my ranch and they had my family, what could I do?" So, that is the situation I don't know what part he played in it. There is no doubt of the part Shinohara, Swada, and Dejima played. Mrs. Sawada was very much in evidence in the hospital and the whole place after they took it over. She came to us and demanded blankets and bedclothing for the Japanese officers who were quartered at her house. She took a truck and went through the whole of the island. She had been there a long enough that she knew most of the natives. She took what she wanted out of their homes. They took livestock, caribou, cattle, all that sort of thing, loaded it on ships and took it to Japan. Some of it they slaughtered on the island and some of it I think they took alive. Another measure which the Japanese had instituted was control of all of the island's food resources. They had required each storekeeper, it made no difference how minor he was, to list all of his supplies, everything was rigidly controlled by the Japs. I stood in the ward of the hospital and watched the natives stand in the hot sun, and it gets hot in Guam, for hours and hours waiting to get permission to buy even a pound of rice. I don't know that many of them had very much in the way of food by the time we left after the Japanese had stripped them of all the things that they wanted. I understand that the Japanese put in a little more agriculture than the natives had been accustomed to cultivate under our regime there. I imagine that quite a few of them got acquainted with a rice paddy who hadn't known anything about rice paddies before.

One of the incidents which always stands out in my mind was one hot sunny day when I saw the Japanese march all of our prisoners up the hill toward the officer's club. None of us trusted the Japanese, we didn't know what was going to be our ultimate disposition, and I think none of us would have been at all surprised to have been lined up and shot. Only I later learned the Japanese use bayonet for those things rather than a shot, it doesn't waste ammunition. Anyway, they lined up all of the officers and marched them up the hill to the officer's club and after they were up there a while we heard firing. I think we lived almost an eternity in that length of time until we finally saw them winding down the hill again, the officers and men. Later we heard that the Japanese had taken them on maneuvers, in other words, they had taken them up to show off. Our turn came some time later when we were informed that all of the Navy nurses and any of the native nurses, who could be spared from the hospital wards were to report.

1016

We reported and assembled in the plaza and watched a review of the Japanese. I tried at that time to determine whether they were running the same equipment around time after time or if they really had that much equipment on the island. At that time one Jap looked just like another to me and I couldn't tell the difference. They had, however, considerable anti air-craft equipment on the island. They had a full troop of cavalry. What in the world they thought they were going to do with cavalry in Guam I don't know, but they had them there. After this review, we were taken up the hill to the officer's club where the Japanese proceeded to demonstrate some of their military tactics, their machine guns and their flame throwers, and their tactics in taking a position, that sort of thing. The idea, of course, being to show off and to let us know their supposed military might, I don't think anybody was awfully impressed, though naturally we didn't make any comment about it. On the way back after a while I was very much struck with the idea that coming down the hill we walked something like a goosestep and I made the comment to Governor, Capt. Geo. McMillan, USN, that I never expected to learn the goosestep, but it looked like I would be learning it under the Japanese military. Anyway that was the end of the review.

During the time that we were on the island a number of the officers were repeatedly questioned by the Japanese. I was very much amused at the Governor's attitude. At any time the Japanese questioned him he informed them immediately that he would give them any information they desired about the civil administration on the island, but as for military affairs, as a Naval Officer, international law did not require that he give out any military information and he would not do so. To every question that came up of a military nature he simply answered - "I don't know." One Japanese commander in the Navy, in particular, made himself very obnoxious, and I think that practically every officer who met him hopes that he will get a chance at him some day. Anyway, in the case of the Governor's questioning when he had repeatedly answered - "I don't know." the officer who was interrogating him said - "How can it be that a man who seems to know as little as you say you know can have attained to the position which you hold?" To which the Governor very laconically answered - "I don't know." We were very much amused - I think they got just about as much information out of everybody else in the place.

In one of the sessions of questioning the Japanese held with the Governor of the island, Captain McMillan, the question that came up was "Who is Commander of the Asiatic Fleet?" To which, the Captain answered - "Don't you know? the Navy has an Admiral out there, we think he is pretty good, we've kept him on two years past his retirement age. His name is Hart. If you don't know him I think you will meet him soon." Another question was - "Who is in charge of the Army in the Philippines?" To which, the Governor answered - "I don't know much about the Army. They have a General out there that they are rather fond of. They have kept him on past his retirement age too. His name is MacArthur. He is probably another one of the people you will meet."

Time went on and the rumor which had been circulating that we were leaving became more persistent and on the 9th of January we were moved from our quarters into those with the native nurses and on the 10th of January we were hastily summoned. We knew that something was going on because the night before the doctors and the hospital corpsmen who had been assigned for the maintainence of the hospital were taken over to the Church with the rest of the prisoners so we realized that we were ready for a move. On the 10th we were loaded with our luggage onto the top of a truck and rode down to Piti to the Navy Yard. One instance and one man stand

1017

out among the Japanese. At the time the Japanese had landed, when they first came onto the hospital compound one of the Japanese interpreters had come up to our Captain and said to him that he was so sorry that war had come between Japan and the United States: that his home had been in the United States for 18 years, his wife and family were still here; that he had been very well treated; his life in the United States had been happy, but he had gone back to Japan for a visit with his family and because of his dual citizenship had been inducted into the Japanese army before he could get out of the country. That man had done, in everything that he could, to make things smoother, he couldn't do a lot, but I think that he had kept us, in our quarters, from a lot of the unpleasantness that might have come to us; first of all the Japanese would come trailing in at all hours and finally a stop was put to it and a notice was posted on our quarters to the effect that only people who had business there or were of officer rank would be admitted, and I think it was due to this man that we received the very small amount of consideration that we did receive. Anyway, when we were loaded onto this pickup truck sitting on our suitcases on our way to Piti he had come by to inquire if we were all right and, of course, we were. The men were required to march the five miles from Agana to Piti. The patients were taken from the hospital with the exception of two, Blaha, a Chief Yeoman who had had machine gun and bayonet wounds. He had been wounded by a machine gun at the taking of the island when a Japanese commanded him to get up and he said he couldn't the Japanese had stuck a bayonet in his chest. The other patient was Perry, who was manager of the cable station and who had a paralysis due to a bomb fragment in his spine. These were just a couple of examples of the casualties. I, myself, saw the bodies of the American Marines being brought in. I said to the corpsment later who was in the morgue at the time they came in following the invasion - "What wounds were on those bodies?" and he said - "Bayonet wounds." I said - "I thought so." They were bayonet wounds in the back. The men who had surrendered had been required to strip off all of their clothing except shorts, had been searched, evidently had been required to kneel at the feet of the Japanese and had been bayoneted in the back. That was typical. Any of the natives that had gotten in their way had been bayoneted without regard to age, sex or color. And so, the general stay on the island had been chaotic and confused. We didn't know what was coming to us, and we didn't know where we were going.

We were loaded aboard the ARGENTINA MARU. The men were carried in a cargo hold of the ship down below the water line. The patients were put in a twelve man steward's cabin and some of the hospital corpsmen were there. The nurses and the wife of a chief petty officer and her six weeks old baby was the only other white woman remaining on the island, were put in to a four berth stewardess' cabin. The traveling arrangements, of course, were such that two of us had to sleep on the deck each night, but the deck being Japanese Tatami was just about as soft as Japanese mattress on the bunks so nobody objected very much or even thought much about it. The food here during the five days that we were aboard ship was rice, or spagetti, or something of that sort. The rice was full of weevils. We got in to Japan on the 15. We cast anchor in the morning. We had two slices of bread for breakfast. The heat went off, the crew left the ship, and nothing happened. The day wore on. After nightfall we were taken up on deck and from there were put aboard a barge which nearly upset in the process of loading. The blankets which had been issued for the patients while aboard ship had been taken from them, and they were brought aboard the barge some covered only with sheets.

About six feet out from the wall in each of these rooms was a light padding of straw with a straw mattress thrown over it. These were the beds of the hospital patients, in fact, the beds of most of the prisoners during the first days in the prison camp. The patients were put down on the beds and some of the Japanese bustled around getting blankets for them. A Japanese second lieutenant came in a pointed to one section of the room and said - "Patients here." and then he pointed to the other and said - "Nurses here." We sort of stood aghast for a minute and then we said - "No." For a minute we were too stunned to say anything. Then he said - "Yes, Patients here and nurses here." We said - "Well, we don't sleep with our patients, we have a hospital corps detachment who can sleep here without any embarassment and American nurses don't sleep in the same rooms with their patients and share quarters with them." Well, anyway, after considerable argument the Colonel came in and he said - "Patients here and nurses here." and we said - "No." He stamped his foot and walked out, and we still said - "No." So, the Second Lieutenant left. Five females who jabbered English much faster than he could understand it, though he spoke English, was too much for even a Jap. He came back eventually and directed us to another room which was a little bit off, at least, it had partitions in it, where we could have a little amount of privacy and the hospital corpsmen shared the rooms with the patients. None of the patients were seriously ill, they didn't require skilled nursing care. They had been a month in the hospital in Guam and during that time the ones who were going to die had died, and the others had reached the stage of convalescence where they required dressings and they required help in getting around but they weren't running elevations of temperature and they were not seriously ill. That was ou introduction to the Japanese prison camp. The camp was an old Army barracks, unheated, dimly lighted, and dirty. Wings branched off from the central building and the rooms were arranged in succession down the length of the wings, a center corridor running the full length of the wing. Incidentially, the day we landed in Japan there was a high wind and snow, and all of the Americans were very cold. Once ashore the patients, nurses, Mrs. Hillmers and her baby were loaded into ambulances and buses for the ride to the prison camp. The remainder of the prisoners were greeted formally by the Military Commandant, loaded onto the street cars, and came to the camp much later.

Mrs. Hillmers, her baby, and the Bishop and Brother Jesus (both Spanish) were taken to the village inn for lodging. At about 9:30 the rest of the prisoners came to the camp. We had had nothing to eat you remember but two slices of bread since morning. After we had been there a while they brought in a bucket of something hot. We read in the newspapers the next day that it was cabbage soup. We never did know what was supposed to be in it, anyway, it steamed, and some bread. So, we ate the bread and we ate some of the so-called cabbage soup. By this time they had issued some blankets to us. Now, don't get any ideas about these blankets. It sounds wonderful, but they were Japanese staple fiber which has a basis of wood. It has a lot of weight but no particular warmth. I know that all of us put all five blankets on the places that we were sleeping, pulled off our shoes and with all the rest of our clothes crawled under a double thickness of all five blankets, and I know that I shivered until morning, and I think that everybody else did. I have never been so cold in my life. We had two meals the next day, rice and soup. But a volunteer crew of our own people, two officers and a number of enlisted men, agreed to take over the galley which was on the prison camp grounds, after cleaning the place up from the results of it's long neglect they started cooking whatever food the Japanese issued and after that we had three meals a day.

Rice was issued twice a day, bread once a day. The rice had wheat germ mixed with it in order to make up the vitamin B1 content which is lost in the polishing of rice. In addition to this, they issued a small quantity of vegetables which in order to go around at all had to be cooked in a large quantity of water and which they designated as soup.

After we had been in the camp for several days, about 10 I think, the civilians among us were moved to Kobe. Mrs. Hillmers and the baby, the Bishop and Brother Jesus, were taken along. After about three weeks of this crowded living condition in the camp the Japanese decided that we ought to have more room and that they would open another barracks. They did this and built up from the floor a platform on which they placed hard packed straw mattresses and these were our beds. They were not a whole lot more comfortable than the floor had been but at least it was more convenient to keep the place in order and to keep it clean. Life settled down pretty much to a routine in the camp there. The Japanese started classes in Japanese and many of the officers and men attended. I think they probably thought they might get back into the fight someday and would use some of the same tactics on the Japs that the Japs had tried to use on us. At any rate, other classes were started too, some of the officers had started classes in mathematics and various things for the men hoping that by teaching them they would be able to qualify for higher rates when they got out of prison camp and it would serve also to keep these things clear in the minds of the men who were teaching so that they wouldn't lose their touch with things. The question of our status as non-combatants had come up and the Japanese had said that even though we were non-combatant, the doctors and nurses and hospital corps, should they be released they would be of service with a combat unit and, therefore, they would not be released but would be retained at the camp. So we were more or less settled down for the duration. The general attitude of the men at the camp was excellent. They never lost their sense of humor, a thing which the Japanese couldn't understand and they watched with considerable suspicion during the early days at the camp because they thought we knew something of a military nature that was going to be sprung as a surprise to them. The men were questioned here, many of the officers, were questioned here at the camp again and their status determined. After they had been there a while, as I say, things had settled down and the classes had started, and the discipline and the morale was good. It more or less settled down on the same lines of discipline that you would find in a Naval establishment anywhere. The five of us, not having any nursing duties since there were no seriously ill patients, devoted ourselves to the business of keeping the existing clothing supply in order. I never knew there were so many buttons until I got to Zentsuji which is the prison camp. Most of the men had come off with not much more than they wore on their backs, and through the Embassy group from Tokyo had been able to send up a few things through the Swiss, it was not anything near an adequate supply of clothing. The attitude of the officers at the camp was good. The Americans had realized, of course, that there was nothing that they could do about it, they were in a bad spot, they were prisoners of war, and so they maintained discipline among themselves and they maintained discipline among the men. They kept their barracks in good order and their dress in good order, and as a result, the Japanese were quite pleased because every time some big wig of their army came to inspect, the General who was commanding the place was commended for the condition of neatness of it and as a result he seemed to feel rather kindly toward the men who were imprisoned there. I didn't see any instances of any brutality at the camp. There might have been some and those things were kept from us, I don't know, I didn't see any.

We were very much surprised after having been told by the Japanese that we were military and would be retained there to be told, about the middle of March, that we were being moved to Kobe. We weren't awfully keen on this Kobe move because we didn't know exactly what Kobe held. It was sort of a "Better the evil that you know, than the evil that you know not." At least, we were with our own people at Zentsuji, and we knew what Zentsuji was like. However, we had no choice, I assure you, and found ourselves on the 13th of March in Kobe. The man who met us in Kobe was a Japanese who spoke excellent English. He had spent many years, I think, in the United States, I don't believe he was American born but he certainly was American educated, at least in part. He was working with the Japanese immigration office, and throughout our whole stay at the detention house in Kobe he was considerate of us and went out of his way to do many things that were nice to us. I think that his people too were still in the United States, and he realized that they would receive decent treatment at our hands and was trying in his own way to give us the sort of treatment he felt his own people were getting.

The detention house, the eastern lodge, had been an old hotel which had been frequented by Indians and the manager was an Indian too. India, of course, was not in the war against the Japanese and these people though they were not restricted, at least nominally they were not restricted, there was still some restriction and they were under constant suspicion. The people at the detention house, other than ourselves, were Dutchmen mainly who had been business representatives of various branches in Japan and Japanese territory, and then after we were there sometime ten missionary priests and an American Protestant missionary were added to our community. Late more Allied Nationals came. That all helped considerably because after all they were our own people and the priests having been a long time in Japan were allowed to bring some of their books with them. The conditions of life at the detention house were considerably better than they had been at the camp. There was more variety of food and better food. We had beds to sleep on and there was hot water so that we could have a shower. The hot water was on about two or three hours during the morning, and we could get laundry done and things of that sort during that period. The house was unheated and we sat around in all the clothes we could find to put on most of the time. We got there in winter and it was rather cold. We didn't have the restrictions there, there was much less tension at the eastern lodge than we had had before.

We had, as I said before, books to read. One of the Dutchmen had been allowed to bring a phonograph and some records, which helped. His records were widely selected with quite a range of types of music and it helped a lot. There were a number of people who spoke other languages. Some of us studied languages. We had, of course, our household duties too. We were particularly fortunate, I think, there in having an amah who was a Japanese woman and had been in charge of buying the food during the time the lodge was a hotel, and she seemed to consider it a matter of pride to provide as well as she could for us in order that when we came home we might not be able to say too many adverse things about her country. She felt that we were foreigners within their midst and that they should put a foot foremost. She was very considerate in many instances. Our guard here, the man in charge of the place, had been a Japanese policeman and was probably called back to active service, and then they had some members of the Japanese police. Some of them were cantakerous and some of them were thoughtful, you didn't know exactly when you made a request what response you were going to get. We were permitted during the time we were in Kobe to go shopping on a couple of occasions. The Swiss had come and we were able to get a very limited amount of funds but, at least, we could buy some hose of which we were in desperate need, and we had

1021

gotten a few other supplies that we needed on these times when we had gone shopping. On occasions we commented that we didn't get enough exercise, because it was rather a confined place. There was a small plot of ground around this hotel which the earlier internees had converted into a garden. They planted some vegetables and some flowers and so on outthere, and it was green and nice but it was very small. It certainly didn't allow for any degree of exercise, so the Japanese decided that they would let us get some exercise and they took us for long walks in the surrounding territory with a couple of guards and attendants. I think the first walk was something like seven or ten miles. After not having any amount of exercise for a while I can assure you that we all had some stiff sore muscles for a couple of days. Life was reasonably uneventful here, except for one thing. That was Doolittle's raid. One of the priests and I had been in the garden and we heard the planes come over and we hadn't heard any Japanese planes for some time, and so we looked them over pretty carefully and decided between us that they weren't Japanese, they were probably our own. Our suspicions were soon confirmed when one of the planes separated from the others and dropped bombs on the docks in Kobe and then joined the other two on the way over to Osaka. The effect of this raid, whatever it might have been from a military point of view, had quite an effect on Japanese morale because just about two weeks previous to that one of their military spokesman hat gotten up and sounded off to the effect that Japan could not be raided by an outside power, and here was an outside power showering them that day with bombs and showing them it could be done. We didn't know that it was General Doolittle until we were on the way home, but whoever it was - the bombing was certainly a welcome visitor as far as we were concerned.

There had been a persistent rumor there was going to be an exchange of prisoners. We had the English version of the Japanese newspapers, the Osaka Mainichi, but, of course, that was a prepared version and was often times very different from the Japanese version. However, some of the people with us had been many years in Japan and they would get the Japanese version from the guards and compare them, so between the two versions and what we knew of the situation we had a reasonably good source of information. I am quite sure that the Japanese didn't realize how much information we actually got out of it, or they wouldn't have allowed us to have the newspapers. Their propaganda is something that is unbelievable. In all the time that I was in Japan they sank our fleet I think a total of six or seven times as reported in their public press. I never saw them actually admit a loss of their own in their press. Occasionally, a plane would fly off into the distance or something of that sort, but they never lost anything, so I was much surprised when I saw Tojo's announcement of their losses the first year of the war. If he announced that loss then they must have had a terrifically greater loss than was announced judging by the general Japanese propaganda attitude.

Finally, it became very definite that there would be an exchange of nationals. The five of us did not expect, however, to be exchanged. We were military personnel, and we had no expectation of coming back. However, a few days before the Swiss had come to us, this same Japanese interpreter had told us confidentially that at least the five of us were going to be exchanged, but that Mrs. Hillmers was not on the list. We couldn't quite understand that, but it seems the Japanese attitude was that inasmuch as her husband was still in Japan she would want to remain there too. Well, anyway, the English woman, who had been many years in Japan and who was interned with us and was more or less responsible for us, finally got things straightened out and Mrs. Hillmers was put on the list. Then the Swiss consul came and notified us officially that we were all on the list to go home. Of all the ironic things, the customs people examined our luggage before we could leave and, by the way, we had had a customs examination at the prison camp, if you please, prisoners of war stripped of everything the Japanese wanted, and the customs officials had given us their OK. Anyway, the same man who examined my luggage at Zentsuji had examined it in Kobe, and since I didn't have anything that he could possibly want anyway, why, we all got through. We went from Kobe - we were taken on a day coach to Yokohama and then we were taken down to Tokyo for breakfast and back to Yokohama when we went aboard the ASAMA MARU. Once aboard we found that we had been assigned very nice quarters. We hadn't expected that we would have them but later one we found out that the American diplomatic corps had had the arranging of quarters on the ship, and that the men had given up their first class accomodations in order that the women passengers of the group might have good accomodations, and Mr. Dooman who was the counsellor of the Embassy laughingly said - "You were the first people that were taken care of, we thought after you had had as many weeks as you had had in Japan that you deserved at least a good place to sleep." Anyway, the State Department in all respects was very helpful to us. We were aboard a couple of days, no, the next day in fact, when we met the Naval Attache from Tokyo, Commander Smith-Hutton, to whom we gave our report, and he was extremely thoughtful to us and many of the things that needed straightening out were straightened out for us by the Naval Attache and the State Department.

The ship moved out into the harbor and we just sat there. Nobody knew what the holdup was, we sort of wondered if we were going back to Japan or if we were going home at all, or were just going to sit in Yokohama Harbor for the duration, and we sortof wondered if the food was going to hold out, or if there were any fish in Yokohama Bay that we might entice onto a line to supplement the food supply. Anyway on the 25 of June we did get underway. We had just about decided that we were going to stay there for the duration. We did not trust the Japanese, and we had an uneasy feeling. Miss Christiansen and myself turned in rather early, and Miss Fogarty who was more of a night owl than we came tearing in and said - "Get awake, you two, we're underway." Well, it didn't take us long to get the sleep out of our eyes when we had that word, and we rushed to the porthole and looked out and reflected on the waters of Yokohama Bay was the huge cross which marked our ship as the diplomatic one. We faced the sea with a great deal of pleasure, but we weren't sure even yet. We weren't sorry to see the shores of Japan receding. We came home pretty well stripped of everything that we possessed. We were not allowed to bring any American money out with us. The American money that some of the people had been able to take in to Japan, the Japs had offered at a rate of exchange of one for one. We were allowed to bring out a limited amount of yen. However, none of us had any more than that because the only amount of yen that we had been able to get was the very small amount from the Swiss Consul.

We left Yokohama the 25th of June and from there we went on down past Formosa to Hong Kong. There we picked up a group of Americans who had been interned at Stanley, and from Hong Kong we went on to French Indo China. We picked up the diplomatic corps there and a group of other people and went from there on down to Singapore. We anchored off Singapore, not in sight of the island. The Japanese were very sure that we didn't see anything going on. The only people who were allowed ashore were some of the Chileans we were bringing home, because Chile at that time had not broken off relations with the Axis. They went into Singapore, and when they returned they wouldn't talk for days on what they had seen there.

From Singapore we went on down through the Sunda Strait between Java and Sumatra, across the Indian Ocean skirting Madagascar and on up to Laurenco Marques. We found the GRIPSHOLM waiting for us there. We left the ASAMA MARU without any trouble, and once ashore on Africa we felt that we were finally free men and women, but life wasn't quite as simple as we thought it might be; we went aboard the GRIPSHOLM only to find that there was the utmost confusion about cabins. One of the nuns found that she had been quartered with one of the men and that sort of thing. For three days I didn't have any place to sleep nor did many others, and that was the general situation. It seems as though some people, some experts in berthing, had come over to Laurenco Marques to berth us all, and they were just a little bit to expert and the result was confusion and chaos.

We finally sailed after we had been there I think about four days, and once out to sea we finally got shaken down into some sort of quarters. The ship came down around the Cape and up across the South Atlantic to Rio. At Rio we discharged the South American members of our passenger list. It has been an extremely interesting group of people because we had the diplomatic representatives of North and Central and South America there. We had an assortment of missionaries and business people and some of the foreign correspondents. It was an excellent opportunity for practical application of the good neighbor policy. It was my first lengthy contact with any Latin American people and I found it extremely interesting. They were, almost without exception, excellent representatives of their country abroad. Rio is truly a beautiful city, many people have said that it is one of the three most beautiful ports in the world, and I will certainly never argue with them. It is one of the most beautiful places I have ever seen, but I assure you that nothing has ever looked so good to me as the Statue of Liberty in New York Harbor.

Once docked, we were home, we were back in the hands of the Navy. Of course, there was the little item about our getting back into the States. While the four of us had been in Guam, I forgot to tell you that all five of us didn't come home, Miss Fogarty, left us at Laurenco Marques, and she was married to Frederick Mann of the State Department and she went on to Brazzaville, but the rest of us came home. We had no passports when we went out to Guam, since that was a part of our own country. So, we wondered if we were going to have to go to Ellis Island while we proved that we were American citizens. However, immigration said they would waive the passports if the State Department would vouch for us, and the State Department said - Well, they knew who we were even if immigration didn't, so we got in. After we docked we had a little session with the FBI and ONI and the Army Intelligence and a few other people and I know that I, and I think most of the rest of them assumed that our report had already been given to the Naval Attache from Tokyo, Commander Smith-Hutton, and that in the event there was anything further we would contact the Office of Naval Intelligence. So, without much ado we got ashore thanks to Commander Smith-Hutton who had engineered it so successfully for us. We were back then in America and glad to be back.

There are a number of things that I observed about the Japanese. I think that they have staked practically everything on this war, and I think they realize it and they realize that if they lose they are lost for a long time. It is going to be a nasty fight, and it is going to be a dirty fight, because they don't fight according to our rules, they make their own as they go along and they aren't pretty. They are not a nice people to be at war with. It is going to take an awful lot, I think we all know. It is just a dirty job that we have to get done.

1024

If it isn't done now, I feel like I still have to get back and get a few licks in, but, nevertheless, it was good to be back and to see my people. They had had no word from me until I got to Rio. They had had some messages from the Navy Department to the effect that I was a prisoner as soon as the Red Cross had established it. By the way, the Red Cross representative had called at the camp, but he had not called until the day, the 12th of March I believe, the day we were leaving the camp. We had been there since the 15th of January. He had probably had a little difficulty getting permission from the Japanese to visit. That was the one and only time I saw him. He was a Swiss doctor who had spent 25 years in Japan. When we had come through Laurenco Marques I had seen quantities of Red Cross supplies unloaded from the GRIPSHOLM to be re-shipped to Japan and some from the Canadian Red Cross to go to Singapore and Hong Kong. As far as I know the Japanese cleared that which was going to Japan for the American prisoners. They did not clear quite a lot of the stuff, according to my understanding of it, that was to have gone to Singapore and to Hong Kong. For some reason they would not let some of the Canadian stuff go through. Since then we have had word through the Red Cross from some of the people who were there. They have stated that they have received some supplies from the United States.

The military attache who was in Tokyo says that he gets to go in on the first tank that goes into Tokyo. For me, I think, I'll reserve a place on the second - I rate that much anyway.

Index to the Oral History of
Captain Wilma Leona Jackson,
Nurse Corps, U.S. Navy (Retired)

Alcohol
Treatment of an alcoholic patient in the late 1930s at the Philadelphia Naval Hospital, 51-54

Army Air Corps, U.S.
Personnel stationed at Wright Field, near Dayton, Ohio, in the early 1930s, 15-16

Asama Maru
Japanese merchant ship used in 1942 for the repatriation of personnel who had been interned at the beginning of World War II, 102-105

Bohlen, Charles
U.S. Foreign Service officer who was interned in Japan at the beginning of World War II and later in his career served as an ambassador overseas, 106-107

Bombing
The Doolittle raid against Japan in April 1942, 74, 101, 103

Brazil
In 1942 the Swedish merchant ship Gripsholm stopped at Rio Janeiro to deliver Latin American diplomats who were being repatriated after having been interned at the outset of World War II, 108

Bureau of Naval Personnel
Role in assigning Navy medical personnel in the 1950s, 31-33; in 1942 received reports on naval personnel captured on Guam the year before, 112

Carter, President James E., Jr. (USNA, 1947)
When Iran seized American hostages in 1979, Carter did not have sufficient understanding of the Muslim culture, 92

Chandler, Quartermaster Clerk Paul G., USMC
Was stationed in China at the outset of World War II but managed to avoid being captured by the Japanese, 102

Chaplain Corps, U.S. Navy
Jackson's involvement with chaplains during the course of her career, 72-75

Chaumont, USS (AP-5)
Navy transport that took Jackson and others from the West Coast of the United States to Guam in 1940-41, 78-79

Christiansen, Lorraine
U.S. Navy nurse who was captured on Guam in 1941 and subsequently repatriated the following year, 111-112

Congress
Involved in giving ranks to members of the Navy Nurse Corps during World War II, 37-38, 41; interest in the 1980s in closing down veterans' hospitals, 50-51

Conte Verde
Merchant ship used in 1942 for the repatriation of personnel who had been interned at the beginning of World War II, 74, 105-106

Dauser, Captain Sue S., NC, USN
Served as director of the Navy Nurse Corps before and during World War II, 37-38, 71, 84, 108-109

Dewitt, Captain Nellie Jane, NC, USN
Served as director of the Navy Nurse Corps in the late 1940s, 41, 72

Doolittle Raid
Bombing of Japan in April 1942, 74, 101, 103

Enlisted Personnel
Role of pharmacist's mates in naval hospitals in the late 1930s, 17-18, 28-29, 34-35, 43-44, 51-54, 65-66; question in the 1950s about the roles of the Nurse Corps and Bureau of Naval Personnel in assigning hospital corpsmen, 31-33; high mortality rate among pharmacist's mates serving with the Marine Corps in World War II, 35-36, 54-55; effects of having a lower pay level than that for officers, 48-50

Families of Servicemen
In the period before World War II, dependents of Navy men often had to get their medical care from civilian hospitals, 46, 48

Fogarty, Virginia
U.S. Navy nurse who was captured on Guam in 1941 and subsequently repatriated the following year, 109-110

Germany
Americans kept track of Adolf Hitler's rise to power in the 1930s through radio, 10-11

Gibson, Captain Winnie, NC, USN
Served as director of the Navy Nurse Corps in the early 1950s, 40

Gripsholm
Swedish merchant ship used in 1942 for the repatriation of personnel who had been interned at the beginning of World War II, 74, 105-106, 108

Guam, Marianas Islands
Used as a staging area for the Marine Corps invasion of Okinawa in 1945, 35-36; logistic support of in the period just before World War II, 61-63; during the early 1940s the Navy ran a school of nursing on the island, 63, 67, 71-72, 76, 80-82, 84-85; treatment provided in the early 1940s by the U.S. medical facilities, 69-70, 82-84, 88, 93; U.S. invasion of in 1944, 75; the island was not fortified against Japanese attack in the years prior to World War II, 79; conditions after U.S. forces recaptured the island in 1944, 81-82, 84-88, 102, 111-112; living and working conditions for U.S. Navy nurses in 1941, 83; in 1941 Japanese military forces invaded and captured the island, 85, 93-96; the son of a Japanese merchant on Guam during World War II subsequently became an American physician, 89-91; after being captured on Guam in 1941, Jackson and other U.S. personnel were prisoners of war, 94-101

Hitler, Adolf
Americans kept track of Hitler's rise to power in the 1930s through radio, 10-11

Houghton, Captain Ruth, NC, USN
Served as director of the Navy Nurse Corps in the late 1950s, 40

Iwo Jima, Bonin Islands
Pharmacist's mates were among the primary targets of the Japanese in 1945 when Marines invaded this island, 54-55

Jackson, Captain W. Leona, NC, USN (Ret.)
Girlhood in Ohio in the 1910s, 1-2, 12, 56-57; education of in Ohio in the 1920s and 1930s, 2, 8; ancestors and other relatives of, 2, 5, 7-13, 56-57, 59, 68, 74-77, 79, 85, 91, 111; training in the 1920s to be a nurse, 2-6, 9, 46-48, 67-68; parents of, 7, 9-12, 14-16; son of, 10, 14-16, 77-78, 100; worked as a civilian nurse in the early 1930s, 13, 17; brief marriage in the early 1930s ended in divorce, 14, 16; as a Navy nurse in Philadelphia and Brooklyn in the late 1930s, 14, 17-28, 42-46, 48-54, 65-66; as director of the Navy Nurse Corps in the 1950s, 31-33, 39-40, 60, 106-107; postgraduate education at Columbia University in the early 1950s, 55-58, 64-65, 91, 96; interest in making clothes, 57-59; served in 1940-41 on the island of Guam, 61-63, 67, 69-72, 76, 80-85, 93-95; return to Guam after the U.S. invasion in 1944, 66, 74, 84-85, 94, 102; duty in Washington, D.C., shortly after World War II, 72-73; repatriation in 1942 from Japan to the United States, 74-75, 102-110; temporary duty at Mare Island in 1940-41, 78-79; after being captured on Guam in 1941, Jackson and other U.S. personnel were prisoners of war, 94-101; activities after returning to the United States in the summer of 1942, 108-113

Japan
Site of internment for nurses, missionaries, and prisoners captured at the beginning of World War II, 74, 98-104; Doolittle bombing raid in April 1942, 74, 101, 103; in 1941 Japanese

forces invaded and captured Guam, 85, 93-96; the son of a Japanese merchant on Guam during World War II subsequently became an American physician, 89-91; after the Japanese captured them on Guam in late 1941, Jackson and other U.S. personnel were prisoners of war, 94-104, 109

Kobe, Japan
Site of internment for nurses, missionaries, and prisoners captured at the beginning of World War II, 74, 101-104

Kreuz, Lieutenant (junior grade) Frank P., MC, USN
Young doctor stationed at the Philadelphia Naval Hospital in the late 1930s, 22, 27, 33-34

Leamer, Lieutenant Robert R., MC, USN
Surgeon who served at naval hospitals in Philadelphia and Brooklyn in the late 1930s, 45-46

Mare Island Naval Hospital, Vallejo, California
Before leaving for duty in Guam, Jackson provided temporary help at the hospital over the holiday period of 1940-41, 78-79

Marine Corps
Used Navy pharmacist's mates with Marine units in the late 1930s, 28-29; high mortality rate among pharmacist's mates serving with the Marine Corps in World War II, 35-36, 54-55; Marines were stationed at the Philadelphia Navy Yard in the late 1930s, 35-36; involvement in the Bougainville operation, 74; Marines wounded, captured, and killed in 1941 during the Japanese conquest of the island of Guam, 93-94; a Marine officer assigned to China at the beginning of World War II managed to escape capture by the Japanese, 102; involved in the recapture of Guam in 1944, 111-112

Medical Corps, U.S. Navy
Very good doctors in the Navy in the late 1930s, 18-20; some Navy doctors have felt threatened by nurses over the years, 40

Medical Problems
Surgery in naval hospitals in the late 1930s, 18-21; cardiac case in the Philadelphia Naval Hospital in the late 1930s, 21-23; value of sulfa drugs in the late 1930s and afterward in preventing infections, 33-35; appendix and orthopedic cases at Philadelphia in the late 1930s, 42; treatment of venereal disease, 43; various operations at Brooklyn around 1940, 43-46; maternity ward work around 1940, 46-48; treatment of an alcoholic patient at Philadelphia, 51-54; treatment of a cardiac patient around 1940, 65-66; treatment shortly before World War II of a Guamanian woman with heart trouble, 70-71; treatment of tuberculosis on Guam in the 1940s, 84; parasite infestations of Guamanians, 86; difficulties experienced in the 1980s by former Navy nurses, 110

Medical Service Corps, U.S. Navy
Role in the overall Navy medical department over the years, 30-31

Mozambique
   The port of Lourenço Marques was used in the summer of 1942 as a point of exchange for interned personnel who were being repatriated, 105-106

New York Naval Hospital, Brooklyn
   Treatment of elderly veterans in the late 1930s, 21; various surgical operations in the period around 1940, 43-46, 61; role of nurses in the maternity ward, 46-47; description of the physical facilities, 60; treatment of a cardiac patient around 1940, 65-66; replaced during the 1940s by St. Albans Naval Hospital on Long Island, 76

Nurse Corps, U.S. Navy
   Size and status of in the late 1930s, 17; adopted the same uniform as the WAVES after World War II, 23-24; as director in the 1950s, Jackson was concerned about the Nurse Corps having a say in the assignment of hospital corpsmen, 31-33; Navy nurses didn't get actual military ranks until World War II, 37-39; selection of captains in the 1950s, 39-40

Nursing
   Training for the profession in Ohio in the 1920s, 2-6, 9, 46-48, 67-68; taught in Germany in the 19th century, 3; confidentiality concerning patients, 5-6; Jackson's work in the early 1930s as a civilian nurse, 13, 17; in naval hospitals in the late 1930s, 14, 17-28, 33-35, 42-47, 51-54, 61, 65-66; orientation programs for new Navy nurses in the late 1930s, 23-24, 27-29, 45; training in the use of sulfa drugs in the late 1930s, 33-35; during the early 1940s the Navy ran a school of nursing on the island of Guam, 63, 67, 71-72, 76, 80-82, 84-85; development of the nursing profession in the early 1940s, 63-64; treatment provided in the early 1940s by the naval hospital on Guam, 69-71

Pay and Allowances
   Effect on enlisted personnel in having a lower pay level than that for officers, 48-50

Philadelphia Naval Hospital
   Nursing staff in the late 1930s, 14, 17-18; role of pharmacist's mates, 17-18, 28-30; surgery in the late 1930s, 18-21; cardiac case in the late 1930s, 21-23; treatment of veterans, 21-23, 27-28; housing for nurses, 25; introduction of sulfa drugs in the late 1930s, 33-35; appendix and orthopedic cases in the late 1930s, 42; treatment of an alcoholic patient, 51-54

Prisoners of War
   After the Japanese captured them on Guam in late 1941, Jackson and other U.S. personnel were prisoners of war, 94-101

Promotion of Officers
   Captains were a rare breed in the Navy Nurse Corps in the 1950s, 39-40

Pugh, Rear Admiral Herbert Lamont, MC, USN
    Served as the Navy's Surgeon General in the early 1950s, 17, 106-107; as a young surgeon in the Philadelphia Naval Hospital in the late 1930s, 18-21, 34-35; served as a reference for a Japanese man who wanted to become a doctor, 90

Radio
    Broadcasts in the 1930s enabled Americans to keep track of Adolf Hitler's rise to power in Germany, 10-11

Ryan, Commander Frank W., MC, USN
    Surgeon who served at naval hospitals in Philadelphia and Brooklyn in the late 1930s, 45-46

Selection Boards
    Process for choosing captains in the Navy Nurse Corps in the 1950s, 39-40

Training
    For civilian nurses in Ohio in the 1920s, 2-6, 9, 46-48, 67-68; orientation programs for Navy nurses and pharmacist's mates in the late 1930s, 23-24, 27-29, 33-35, 43-44, 65-66; during the early 1940s the Navy ran a school of nursing on the island of Guam, 63, 67, 71-72, 76, 80-82, 84-85

Uniforms-Naval
    After World War II, Navy nurses adopted the same uniform as WAVES, 23-24; not until World War II did Navy nurses get to wear officer insignia on their uniforms, 37-39

Venereal Disease
    Treatment of by Navy medical personnel in the 1930s and 1940s, 43

Veterans Administration
    Some veterans were treated in naval hospitals in the late 1930s, before the VA had its own complex of hospitals, 21-23, 27-28

WAVES
    After World War II, Navy nurses adopted the same uniforms that WAVES had been wearing, 23-24; were regarded during World War II as only temporarily part of the Navy, 37

Women
    See: Nurse Corps, U.S. Navy; WAVES

Wright Field, Dayton, Ohio
    Personnel stationed at this Army Air Corps base in the 1930s, 15-16

Yetter, Doris
    U.S. Navy nurse who was captured on Guam in 1941 and subsequently repatriated the following year, 112

Zentsuji, Japan
　Site of internment for nurses, missionaries, and prisoners captured at the beginning of World War II, 74, 98-101, 103-104, 109

www.ingramcontent.com/pod-product-compliance
Lightning Source LLC
Chambersburg PA
CBHW080611170426

43209CB00007B/1402